MICHIGAN

COOK BOOK

Compiled by
Donna Goodrich

GOLDEN WEST☼ PUBLISHERS

ISBN # 1-885590-29-6

Printed in the United States of America

5th printing © 2004

Golden West Publishers
4113 N. Longview Ave.
Phoenix, AZ 85014, USA
(800) 658-5830

For free sample recipes and complete Table of Contents for every Golden West cookbook, visit our website: **goldenwestpublishers.com**

Table of Contents

Table of Contents (continued)

Side Dishes

Breads & Muffins

Desserts & Snacks

Welcome to Michigan!

For over four centuries, this gem of the upper Midwest has been a haven for those seeking peace, serenity and untouched natural splendor. Surrounded by four of the five Great Lakes, and home to more than 11,000 inland lakes, Michigan boasts more miles of freshwater shoreline than any other state. These vast natural wonders have attracted a wide range of settlers and visitors to Michigan since before the colonial period. From this extensive history comes a cultural legacy, and the finest collection of recipes, contributed by the residents of Michigan, that you will find anywhere.

Enjoy these tastes of Michigan!

Michigan Facts

Size — 23rd largest state with an area of 58,527 sq. miles
Statehood — January 26, 1837 — 26th state
State Nickname — The Wolverine State
Highest Elevation — Mount Arvon, 1,979 ft.
State Tree — White Pine
State Bird — Robin
State Fish — Brook Trout
State Flower — Apple Blossom
State Stone — Petoskey
State Gem — Isle Royale Greenstone
State Song — *Michigan, My Michigan*
State Population — (1998 est.) 9,594,300

Famous People from Michigan

AUTHORS
Edna Ferber-Kalamazoo
M.F.K. Fisher-Albion
William X. Kienzle-Detroit
Terry McMillan-Port Huron

BUSINESS & INDUSTRY
William E. Boeing-Detroit
John & Horace Dodge-Niles
Henry Ford-Dearborn
John Harvey Kellogg-Tyrone
W. K. Kellogg-Tyrone
William E. Upjohn-Richland

MUSIC
Anita Baker-Detroit
Alice Cooper-Detroit
Glenn Frey-Detroit
Berry Gordy-Detroit
Bill Haley-Highland Park
Casey Kasem-Detroit
Madonna-Bay City
Ted Nugent-Detroit

Iggy Pop-Ann Arbor
Della Reese-Detroit
Martha Reeves-Detroit
Diana Ross-Detroit
Smokey Robinson-Detroit
Bob Seger-Dearborn
Stevie Wonder-Saginaw

POLITICAL
Thomas E. Dewey-Owosso
Perle Mesta-Sturgis
Charles Lindbergh-Detroit

SPORTS
Kirk Gibson-Pontiac
George ("Win one for the
Gipper") Gipp-Laurium
"Magic" Johnson-Lansing
Sugar Ray Robinson-Detroit
John Smoltz-Warren

STAGE, FILM & TV
Sandra Bernhard-Flint
Sonny Bono-Detroit

Francis Ford Coppola-Detroit
Pam Dawber-Farmington Hills
Dick Enberg-Armada
Charlton Heston-St. Helen
Kim Hunter-Detroit
Betty Hutton-Battle Creek
Lee Majors-Wyandotte
Ed McMahon-Detroit
Harry Morgan-Detroit
Michael Moriarty-Detroit
George Peppard-Detroit
Gilda Radner-Detroit
Jason Robards, Sr.-Hillsdale
Steven Seagal-Detroit
Tom Selleck-Detroit
Sinbad-Benton Harbor
Tom Skerritt-Detroit
Danny Thomas-Deerfield
Marlo Thomas-Detroit
Lily Tomlin-Detroit
Robert Wagner-Detroit

Michigan Visitor Information: 1-800-543-2937
National Forest Information: U. S. Forest Service 1-800-280-2267
Recreation, Fishing & Hunting Information: 1-517-373-1214
Visit Michigan's Internet Site: .... http://www.michigan.org

Fried Mushrooms

Mary Jo Henrickson—Elmhurst Bed & Breakfast, Shelby

1 stick BUTTER
1 EGG
1 cup BUTTERMILK
1 lb. fresh MUSHROOMS, washed
1 1/2 cups FLOUR
SALT and PEPPER to taste

Melt butter in a medium skillet. Whip egg and buttermilk together. Roll mushrooms in egg mixture, then in flour. Fry in butter, turning until nicely browned on all sides. Season generously with salt and pepper. Drain on paper towels and serve hot.

Serves 6-8.

Smoked Whitefish Dip

"This tasty dip may be served either warm or cold."

Kate & Barbara Vilter—The Riverside Inn
(Chef Thomas Sawyer), Leland

4 oz. CREAM CHEESE (at room temperature)
1/4 cup SOUR CREAM
1 med.-size smoked WHITEFISH TAIL, deboned
1 tsp. PICK-A-PEPPER® SAUCE
1 dash HOT SAUCE (Melinda's® Hot Sauce is recommended)
1 pinch CAYENNE PEPPER
1/4 tsp. SALT
1/4 sweet ONION, finely minced
1 tsp. fresh GARLIC, minced
1/2 tsp. DIJON MUSTARD
1 Tbsp. OLIVE OIL

Combine all ingredients in a blender. Blend until smooth. To serve hot dip, spread the dip in an 8-ounce baking dish. Bake at 350° for approximately 30 minutes, or until warm in the middle and golden on top. Serve with warm bread or sesame crackers. Cold dip is wonderful too, served with fresh vegetables.

Chicken Liver Tidbits

Mary Jo Henrickson—Elmhurst Bed & Breakfast, Shelby

1 lb. CHICKEN LIVERS, rinsed and cut into quarters
1 1/2 cups FLOUR
1 stick MARGARINE
PAPRIKA
SALT and PEPPER to taste

Roll livers in flour. Melt margarine in a medium skillet. Add coated livers and cook over medium heat, turning often, until brown and crispy. Season generously with paprika, salt and pepper.

Serves 4-6.

Stuffed Pea Pods

Flo Schermerhorn—Victorian 1898 Bed & Breakfast, Traverse City

SNOW PEA PODS
1/3 portion BLUE CHEESE
1/3 portion CHEDDAR CHEESE, softened
1/3 portion CREAM CHEESE, softened
MILK or CREAM
PAPRIKA

Use fresh or frozen snow pea pods. Blanch the pods in boiling water for 30 seconds. Drain, rinse in cold water, drain again. Cover and refrigerate. Combine cheeses and milk or cream to a smooth consistency. Cut off stem end of pod diagonally and fill with cheese stuffing, about 1 teaspoon per pod. Sprinkle with paprika. Serve pods as petals of a flower with a fancy radish in the middle. Servings determined by number of pea pods stuffed.

Traverse City

Originally a lumbering town, Traverse City has become the center of a flourishing cherry-growing region as well as a fast-growing wine industry. Positioned at the base of Grand Traverse Bay, Traverse City offers a year-round resort season as well as fishing and sailing in the summer An autumn color trip through Old Mission Peninsula is a must-see adventure.

Dandelion Blossom Fritters

"Simply delicious."

Dorris Stoll—North Adams

Gather **DANDELION BLOSSOMS.** Wash, drain and dry. Dip blossoms in thin **PANCAKE MIX.** Deep fry in **CORN OIL.** Drain on paper towels and serve.

Fried Oysters

Helen Phillips—Charlevoix

12 OYSTERS (1 quart)
1 EGG
2 Tbsp. WATER
1 cup CRACKER CRUMBS, finely crushed
COOKING OIL

Shuck and pat oysters dry with paper towels. Beat egg with water. Dip oysters in egg mixture, then dredge in cracker crumbs. Dip again in egg mixture and again in crumbs. Let dry at least 1/2 hour. Fry until brown, turn and brown the other side. Serve warm.

Cocktail Meatballs with Grape Jam Sauce

"We serve these often when friends and family gather."

Angel Rivera, Saginaw

6 lbs. GROUND BEEF
6 EGGS, beaten
1 Tbsp. CORNSTARCH
SALT and PEPPER to taste
2/3 cup finely chopped ONION

Mix all ingredients together well and form into small meatballs. Brown meatballs in a small amount of oil and drain well on paper towels. Serve warm with ***Grape Jam Cocktail Sauce.***

Grape Jam Cocktail Sauce

1 jar (10 oz.) GRAPE JAM
1 bottle (11 oz.) CHILI SAUCE

Blend together and heat well. Serve warm with meatballs.

Oktoberfest Pretzels

"Pretzels are a favorite of both young and old!"

Peggy L. Reinhardt—Frankenmuth Convention and Visitors
Bureau, Frankenmuth

2 cups MILK	3 Tbsp. SHORTENING
1 cup WATER	9 cups FLOUR
1 cup BEER	1 Tbsp. LYE
1 pkg. YEAST	1 qt. WATER
1 Tbsp. SALT	KOSHER SALT

In a saucepan, combine milk, water and beer. Warm to lukewarm; add yeast, salt and shortening and stir until well dissolved. Add flour in two parts; mix the first 5 cups with a spoon and the last 4 cups by hand. Mix well and let rise for 1 to 1 1/2 hours. Roll out on floured table to pencil-thick ropes and shape into loose knot pretzel shapes. Combine lye* and water in a saucepan and heat to boiling. Reduce to a simmer and maintain simmering temperature while cooking pretzels. Using a slotted spoon, immerse pretzels in lye solution for 1 minute. Place pretzels on a greased baking sheet and sprinkle with kosher salt. Bake in a 450° oven until golden brown. Remove from pan immediately and place on a cooling rack.

Makes about 3 dozen pretzels.

*Lye is very corrosive. Use caution during preparation of pretzels. Refer to lye container for proper handling instructions.

Frankenmuth

In 1845, Bavarian immigrants named their new settlement Frankenmuth, meaning "courage of the Franconians." Visit Bronner's Christmas Wonderland—"The World's Largest Christmas Store." Bronner's is open year round, but at Christmas, displays more than 50,000 ornaments, lights and decorations. Oktoberfest, held in September and Bavarian Festival in June celebrate Frankenmuth's German heritage.

Variety Cheese Balls

1/2 lb. BLUE CHEESE, crumbled
1 cup BUTTER, softened
1 cup finely chopped WALNUTS
3 Tbsp. CREAM
PAPRIKA
finely chopped PARSLEY
finely chopped blanched ALMONDS

In a bowl, combine cheese and butter. Mix well. Stir in walnuts and enough milk to make a smooth mixture. Chill for at least 2 hours. Roll mixture into 1-inch balls. Roll 1/3 of balls in paprika, 1/3 in chopped parsley and 1/3 in almonds.

Marinated Mushrooms

1/2 lb. fresh MUSHROOMS
1 med. ONION, thinly sliced
1/3 cup SALAD OIL
3 drops TABASCO® SAUCE
1 cup TARRAGON WINE
　VINEGAR
1/2 tsp. SALT
fresh PARSLEY, minced

Rinse and pat dry mushrooms. Slice lengthwise through stems and combine with onion in a ceramic or glass bowl. Add balance of ingredients and pour over mushrooms. Stir, cover and let stand at room temperature for at least 4 hours.

Quick 'n Easy Cocktail Sauce

1 cup CHILI SAUCE
1/3 cup HORSERADISH
1/3 cup KETCHUP
1 1/2 tsp. WORCESTERSHIRE SAUCE

Combine and chill mixture thoroughly before serving.

Cherry Sausage

Janet Meteer—Bridgewalk Bed & Breakfast, Central Lake

1 cup TART CHERRIES
2 lbs. LEAN PORK, fat removed, cut into 1" cubes, chilled
2 tsp. SALT
1 tsp. dried SAGE
1/2 tsp. dried THYME
1 1/2 Tbsp. BROWN SUGAR
1/3 tsp. PEPPER

In a food processor, using a metal blade, pulse cherries until finely diced. Set aside in a bowl. In a large bowl, toss cubed pork with remaining ingredients. Divide mixture in half and process with metal blade. Pulse and turn continuously until desired texture is reached. Return to bowl. Add cherries and mix until evenly combined. Refrigerate or freeze until ready to use.

Linda's Apple Pancakes with Fresh Applesauce

"This is my recipe and a favorite here at the Inn. We use apples picked from the trees on the lighthouse grounds."

Linda Gamble—Big Bay Point Lighthouse Bed & Breakfast,
Big Bay

1 cup ROLLED OATS	2 1/4 cups APPLE CIDER
1 cup WHITE FLOUR	3 EGGS
1 cup WHOLE WHEAT FLOUR	2 Tbsp. CANOLA OIL
1 Tbsp. BAKING POWDER	2 lg. APPLES, peeled
3/4 tsp. SALT	and grated
2 Tbsp. SUGAR	

Place uncooked oats in a food processor and process until it is the consistency of flour. In a bowl, combine all the dry ingredients and mix well. Add cider, eggs and oil and mix until moistened. Add grated apple and mix well. Bake on a griddle at 375° until top bubbles and edges are dry. Turn and bake on other side until golden brown. Serve with **Fresh Applesauce.**

Makes 12 pancakes.

Fresh Applesauce

8 lg. APPLES, peeled and sliced	1/4 cup packed BROWN
1/2 cup WATER	SUGAR
1 tsp. CINNAMON	

Place apples and water in saucepan, cover and bring to a boil. Reduce heat and simmer for 10-15 minutes. Add cinnamon and sugar, continue to simmer for 5 minutes. Place in covered bowl and cool in refrigerator before serving.

Overlooking Lake Superior, the Big Bay Point Lighthouse Bed and Breakfast Inn is one of the few surviving resident lighthouses in the country and is listed on the National Register of Historic Places. A trip to the lighthouse lantern, 120 feet above the lake surface, is an essential part of every guest's stay.

Blaney Park Oatmeal

"Blaney Lodge is a restored historical resort in Michigan's Upper Peninsula, near Tahquamenon Falls, Mackinaw Island, and Sault Ste. Marie Locks: 'The place where you can get back to Nature but not be left in the woods'."

Howard Eldridge—Blaney Lodge Bed & Breakfast, Blaney Lodge

1 cup RAISINS
2 cups WATER
3 pinches SALT
2 pinches CINNAMON
1 tsp. VANILLA or 2 tsp. IMITATION VANILLA
1/2 cup ROLLED OATS

In a saucepan, boil 1/2 cup raisins and rest of ingredients (except oats) for about 5 minutes. Let soak 24 hours or longer. Discard raisins and add 1/2 cup fresh raisins. Bring to boil. Add rolled oats. Cook uncovered for 5 minutes, remove from heat, cover and steam for 5 minutes.

Serves 4.

Note: Make leftover oatmeal into patties. Dip patties in whipped eggs, then flour. Fry in butter until brown. Serve with honey or syrup.

Mackinac Island
(pronounced MACK-i-naw)

American Indians called it Michi-limackinac, or "Great Turtle" Island. In 1780 an old French garrison was moved to Mackinac Island by the British and it remained the stronghold of the Straits of Mackinac for 115 years. The island has become a favorite tourist attraction. No motorized vehicles are allowed on the island—transportation is solely by foot, horseback, horsedrawn vehicle or bicycle.

"The Pines" Granola

*"Excellent served with milk or yogurt and fruit,
for breakfast or a snack."*

Donna Hodge—Bed & Breakfast at The Pines, Frankenmuth

4 cups OLD-FASHIONED OATS	3/4 cup BRAN CEREAL
1/3 cup HONEY	1 cup FLAKED COCONUT
1/4 cup OIL	1 cup RAISINS
1 tsp. VANILLA EXTRACT	1 cup chopped DATES
1 tsp. ALMOND EXTRACT	1 tsp. CINNAMON
1 cup chopped PECANS	1 tsp. NUTMEG

Spread oats in a 9 x 12 roasting pan. Bake in a 350° oven
for 5 minutes. Remove from oven and stir. Return to oven for
5 more minutes. In a saucepan, combine honey and oil; heat and
stir until well combined. Remove from heat and cool; stir in
flavorings. Combine the pecans, bran cereal, coconut, raisins
and dates and add to heated oats. Mix thoroughly. Add honey
mixture to oats mixture and combine. Sprinkle cinnamon and
nutmeg over top and return to oven. Bake at 350° for 20 to 25
minutes, stirring every 5 minutes for even browning. Remove
from oven and mix thoroughly. Cool and store in an airtight
container.

Makes about 8 cups granola.

Swiss Eggs

"Our guests often ask for this delicious dish"

Louie & Kathy Weiss—Bavarian Town Bed & Breakfast,
Frankenmuth

Use 5- or 6-inch oval or round ovenproof dishes for each
serving. Spray dishes with nonstick **VEGETABLE SPRAY.**
Layer bottoms with **HAM** slices. Add **2 EGGS.** Add **MUSH-
ROOMS** and **ASPARAGUS** or **BROCCOLI (slightly precooked).**
Cover with **grated BABY SWISS CHEESE.** Add **1 teaspoon
MILK.** Sprinkle with **shredded PARSLEY.** Bake 10-12 minutes
at 350° until set.

Asparagus Eggs Benedict

"The Ludington House hosts Murder Mystery Weekends after the busy tourist season is over. You don't sit and watch; you make it happen! You receive a character assignment in advance with costume suggestions. Once you're there you get the clues to solve the murder. One of you is guilty! It's so much fun, it's almost criminal!"

Virginia Boegner—The Ludington House, Ludington

3/4 lb. fresh ASPARAGUS	1/8 tsp. CAYENNE PEPPER
1/2 cup MARGARINE	3/4 cup shredded CHEDDAR
1/2 cup FLOUR	CHEESE
3 cups MILK	5 hard-cooked EGGS, quartered
1 1/4 cups CHICKEN BROTH	1/2 lb. sliced HAM, cubed
1/2 tsp. SALT	3-4 ENGLISH MUFFINS

Cut asparagus into 1/2-inch pieces. Cook in a small amount of water until it changes color (about 2 minutes), drain and set aside. Melt margarine in a 3-quart saucepan. Stir in flour until smooth. Add milk a little at a time, stirring after each addition until smooth. Add broth, salt, cayenne pepper and bring to a boil; cook and stir for 2 minutes. Add cheese, stirring until it melts. Add eggs, ham and asparagus. Heat through. Serve over toasted English muffins.

Serves 6-8.

Ludington

Situated at the mouth of the Marquette River, Ludington offers safe deepwater harborage in the nearby Pere Marquette Lake. The S. S. Badger, *operated by the Lake Michigan Carferry Service is based here and offers 4-hour cruises and automobile ferry service across the lake to Manitowoc, Wisconsin.*

Farmstead's Country Oatmeal

"This recipe was given to me by a friend, Alma Goozen, years ago. It can be made ahead of time and kept for several days. It reheats well for those hurried breakfast mornings."

Marlene Lipon—Farmstead Bed & Breakfast Ltd., Hartland

4 cups WATER
1/4 tsp. SALT
1 lg. APPLE, peeled, chopped
1/2 cup RAISINS
1/2 cup packed BROWN SUGAR

2 Tbsp. BUTTER
1/2 tsp. CINNAMON
2 1/4 cups QUICK-COOKING OATS
1/2 cup ALMONDS

Place all ingredients except oats and almonds in a large pot and bring to a boil. Add oats and cook over medium heat for 5 minutes. Pour mixture into a buttered 9 x 13 baking pan, sprinkle with almonds and refrigerate. When ready to serve, cut into squares and reheat in oven or microwave. Serve with half and half and sugar.

Serves 6-8.

Michigan Baked Oatmeal

Mrs. Chris Mason—The Parish House Inn, Ypsilanti

2 cups OLD-FASHIONED OATS
1/2 tsp. ALMOND FLAVORING
1/2 cup sliced ALMONDS
1 lg. APPLE, unpeeled, grated

4 cups MILK
1/4 cup packed BROWN SUGAR
1/2 cup dried CHERRIES

Preheat oven to 400°. Coat the insides of a 3-quart casserole or 9 x 13 baking pan with cooking spray. Combine all ingredients in a mixing bowl and mix thoroughly. Transfer to baking dish. Sprinkle top with additional almonds. Bake, uncovered, for 45 minutes. Serve hot.

Variation: Omit almond flavoring and cherries. Add **1 Tbsp. CINNAMON, 1/2 cup RAISINS** and **1/2 cup chopped PEANUTS.**

Serves 4-6

Pannukakku

(Finnish Oven Pancake)

"This was my husband's grandmother's recipe and is frequently served at our bed and breakfast. Pannukakku may be served warm or cold with jam, fruit, honey or syrup."

Charleen Ahola—Creekside Inn Bed & Breakfast, Hancock

1 stick MARGARINE
3 EGGS
3 cups MILK

1 1/2 cups FLOUR
1 tsp. SALT
6 Tbsp. SUGAR

In a 9 x 13 baking pan, melt margarine in a 375° oven. In a bowl, beat eggs well. Add milk alternately with flour. Add salt and sugar. Pour mixture into the hot pan and bake 45 minutes.

Serves 6-8.

Breakfast Pizza

Shirley Piepenburg—Deer Lake Bed and Breakfast, Boyne City

1 pkg. (8 oz.) CRESCENT ROLLS
1 lb. breakfast SAUSAGE
6 oz. (or more) frozen HASH BROWN POTATOES, thawed
1 cup chopped MUSHROOMS
1 ea. RED and GREEN BELL PEPPER, chopped
1 med. ONION, chopped
8 oz. shredded MONTEREY JACK CHEESE
5 EGGS
1/4 cup SKIM MILK
grated PARMESAN CHEESE

Preheat oven to 375°. Spread crescent rolls flat in a greased 9 x 13 pan to form a crust. Fry sausage; drain and crumble on crust. Fry hash brown potatoes until crisp and crumble on top of sausage. Top with the rest of the vegetables and then sprinkle with cheese. Beat eggs and milk together and pour over all. Sprinkle Parmesan cheese over top and bake for 30-35 minutes.

Serves 4.

Blueberry Pancake Squares

Sally Coburn—Fountain Hill Bed & Breakfast, Grand Rapids

1 1/4 cups FLOUR
2 tsp. BAKING POWDER
1/2 tsp. BAKING SODA
1/2 cup WHEAT GERM
1 cup ALL BRAN CEREAL
1 cup BUTTERMILK
1/2 cup ORANGE JUICE
1/4 cup OIL

1/4 cup HONEY
1 Tbsp. grated ORANGE RIND
1/2 tsp. CINNAMON
1 EGG, beaten slightly
1 cup BLUEBERRIES
2 Tbsp. SUGAR
WALNUTS, finely chopped

In a bowl, stir flour, baking powder, baking soda and wheat germ together. In another bowl combine the next 7 ingredients. Let set for 2 minutes. Mix dry ingredients with cereal mixture and spread in a 9 x 13 oiled baking pan. Combine blueberries and sugar and sprinkle on top of batter. Bake at 400° for 20 minutes. Sprinkle top with walnuts. Cut into squares and serve with butter and syrup.

Serves 6-8.

McCann House Baked Oatmeal

"Serve with ice cream for a great dessert too!"

Joyce A. Runberg—Beaver Island

1/3 cup OIL
1/2 cup packed BROWN SUGAR
1 lg. EGG, beaten
2 cups QUICK COOKING OATS
1 1/2 tsp. BAKING POWDER

1/2 tsp. SALT
3/4 cup MILK
CINNAMON to taste
RAISINS to taste

In a medium bowl, combine all ingredients and stir thoroughly. Pour into a greased 9 x 5 loaf pan. Bake at 350° for 25-30 minutes. Serve with milk and sugar.

Serves 6.

Victorian Inn
Apple Pancakes

"This recipe is from the Port City Victorian Inn's favorite fall and winter guest menu. Our guests are served in our dining room or enclosed sunporch. They are delighted that we use Michigan products from our very own farmers' market."

Barbara F. Schossau—Port City Victorian Inn, Muskegon

1 EGG	1/4 cup SUGAR
1 cup BUTTERMILK	1 1/2 tsp. BAKING POWDER
1/4 cup BUTTER, melted	1/2 tsp. SODA
1 cup finely chopped APPLES	3/4 tsp. SALT
1 1/2 cups ALL-PURPOSE FLOUR	1/2 tsp. CINNAMON

Blend egg, buttermilk, butter and apples. Blend dry ingredients together. Add to egg mixture and stir only until dry ingredients are moistened. Grease griddle. To test, sprinkle with drops of water. When water sizzles, griddle heat is just right. Pour batter from pitcher or large spoon in pools slightly apart (for perfectly rounded cakes). Turn pancakes as soon as they are puffed and full of bubbles (before bubbles break). Turn and brown on the other side. Serve immediately with **Maple-Apple Syrup** on the side.

Makes 14 to 16 (4-inch) pancakes.

Maple-Apple Syrup

3 Tbsp. BUTTER	pinch of SALT
1/4 cup chopped PECANS	2 cups peeled and thinly
1 cup MAPLE SYRUP	sliced APPLES
1/2 tsp. CINNAMON	

In a saucepan, melt butter, add nuts and brown lightly. Remove nuts and set aside. Add maple syrup, cinnamon and salt to butter in saucepan. Add apples, cover and simmer slowly for 10 minutes. Stir browned nuts into apple mixture. Pour mixture into a serving pitcher.

Blueberry-Stuffed French Toast

"I originally made just stuffed French toast. But when I moved to Michigan where all the blueberry fields are, I added blueberries to this recipe. My guests just love it!"

Barb Wishon—The Newnham SunCatcher Inn, Saugatuck

1 (1 lb.) loaf FRENCH BREAD, unsliced
1 pkg. (8 oz.) CREAM CHEESE, cubed
1-2 cups BLUEBERRIES
8 EGGS
2 1/2 cups MILK, LIGHT CREAM, or HALF & HALF
6 Tbsp. BUTTER or MARGARINE, melted
1 tsp. CINNAMON
1 Tbsp. VANILLA

Cut French bread loaf into cubes (you should have about 12 cups bread cubes). Grease a 9 x 13 baking dish. Place half of the bread cubes in the baking dish. Top with cream cheese cubes and blueberries and then with the remaining bread cubes. In a large mixing bowl, using a wire whisk, mix together eggs, milk, melted butter or margarine, cinnamon and vanilla, until well combined. Pour egg mixture evenly over top of bread mixture. Using a spatula, lightly press layers down to moisten. Cover with plastic wrap and refrigerate for 2 to 24 hours. Preheat oven to 325° and remove plastic wrap from baking dish. Bake for 35-40 minutes or until center tests set and edges are lightly golden. Let stand about 10 minutes before serving. Serve with warm maple syrup.

Serves 8.

Did you know?

The remains of approximately 80 ship-wrecks may be found in Thunder Bay, near Alpena, making this an excellent diving destination.

Delicious Baked French Toast

"No additional butter or syrup is needed for this moist and flavorful dish."

James Foster—The Roycroft Inn Bed & Breakfast, Mt. Pleasant

1 heaping cup light or dark BROWN SUGAR
1 stick BUTTER
2 Tbsp. light or dark CORN SYRUP or MAPLE SYRUP
1 loaf unsliced BREAD (heavy, dense breads are best)
5 EGGS
1 1/2 cups MILK
1 Tbsp. VANILLA EXTRACT

Slice bread into 3/4-inch slices then cut each slice in half. In a medium saucepan over low heat, mix/melt brown sugar, butter and syrup until it reaches a slow boil. Spray a 9 x 13 baking dish with cooking spray. Pour butter and sugar mixture into baking dish. Layer bread slices over top. In a mixing bowl, blend eggs, milk and vanilla with a whisk until foamy. Pour egg mixture over bread, not missing any areas and using all of the mixture (the excess will be absorbed). Cover baking dish and refrigerate overnight. The next morning, preheat oven to 350°, remove cover from dish, place on middle rack and bake for 30 minutes (top should be a light golden brown when done). Let dish set for a few minutes before serving.

Serves 8.

Roycroft Inn

Roycroft Inn was built in 1877 by Alvin Hobbs, one of the early settlers of Mt. Pleasant. The homestead was a working farm with a blacksmith's shop. In the early 1900s a local judge bought the farm and raised turkeys commercially for many years. The barn and the granary, built in 1877, are open from time to time and house a large quantity of antiques and collectibles.

Peach French Toast Cobbler

"Breakfast receives rave revues when this popular French toast variation is served. This recipe is easy to make and can be prepared ahead of time. It not only smells and tastes great, but is beautiful when presented at the table. Leftovers can easily be reheated for late-sleeping guests. If fresh peaches are not available, substitute frozen ones, or use apples, blueberries or any other fruit, frozen or fresh."

Dave & Jill Wyman—The Hanson House, Grayling

1 (1 lb.) loaf FRENCH BREAD, unsliced
5 EGGS
1/2 cup MILK
1/4 tsp. BAKING POWDER
1 tsp. VANILLA EXTRACT
1/2 cup SUGAR
1 tsp. CINNAMON
1 tsp. CORNSTARCH
4 1/2 cups sliced PEACHES
2 Tbsp. BUTTER, melted
POWDERED SUGAR

Slice bread into eight (3/4- to 1-inch thick) slices; arrange in a shallow baking pan. In a medium bowl, whisk together eggs, milk, baking powder and vanilla. Pour over bread, turning to coat evenly. Cover with plastic wrap and let stand 2 hours at room temperature or overnight in the refrigerator. Preheat oven to 450°. Spray a 9 x 13 baking pan with nonstick cooking spray. Mix sugar (use less if fruits are sweet), cinnamon and cornstarch in a medium bowl; gently fold in peaches until well coated. Spread peaches in prepared pan; place egg-soaked bread, wettest side up, on fruit, wedging slices in tightly. Brush tops of bread with butter and bake 20-25 minutes, or until toast is golden and peaches are bubbling around edge of pan. To serve, place toast on plates; spoon peach sauce from bottom of pan over top and sprinkle with powdered sugar.

Serves 8.

Visit the Icehouse Quilt Shop in Grayling; it was selected as one of the top ten quilt shops in North America.

Harvest Apple Pancakes

"We like to serve these pancakes in the fall when the new crop of apples comes to our fruit markets. They're also wonderfully hearty all through the cold winter months."

Ric and Mary Ellen Postlewaite—Garden Grove Bed & Breakfast,
Union Pier

1 cup FLOUR
2 Tbsp. SUGAR
2 tsp. BAKING POWDER
1/2 tsp. SALT
1/2 tsp. CINNAMON
pinch of NUTMEG

1 EGG
2 Tbsp. CORN OIL
1/2 to 3/4 cup SKIM MILK
1 lg. cooking APPLE, peeled,
   coarsely shredded

Mix dry ingredients. Add egg, oil and milk. Mix briskly by hand until no large lumps remain. Batter should be thin. Add shredded apple and mix thoroughly. Cook on hot griddle. Serve with warm maple syrup and ***Apple Cider Apples*** on the side.

Makes 8 medium-size pancakes.

Apple Cider Apples

1 Tbsp. BUTTER
2 Tbsp. BROWN SUGAR
1/2 cup APPLE CIDER
2 lg. cooking APPLES, peeled and sliced
1 tsp. CINNAMON
1/4 tsp. NUTMEG

Heat butter, sugar and cider in a saucepan until sugar dissolves. Add apples and sprinkle with cinnamon and nutmeg. Simmer gently 5-10 minutes until the apples just start to get tender.

Did you know?

Michigan boasts more than one hundred lighthouses along its shores.

Poached Pears

"The fruits we use are all Michigan products that we get at nearby markets. Our guests love the freshness of the locally grown fruit. I created the following recipes because they lend themselves to a beautiful presentation."

Tom & Gwen Paton—Seymour House Bed & Breakfast,
South Haven

3 fresh PEARS, halved, cored and seeded
4-6 cups WATER
1/3 cup LEMON JUICE

2/3 cup RASPBERRY SYRUP
6 tsp. chopped PECANS
6 MINT LEAVES
POWDERED SUGAR

Place pears in a saucepan with water and lemon juice. Cook very gently until soft but firm. Time varies depending on ripeness of fruit. Place each pear half in a small serving dish and pour syrup over top. Garnish with pecans and a mint leaf. Place serving dish on a 7- or 8-inch clear glass plate that has been sprinkled with powdered sugar.

Serves 6.

Fresh Peaches

Tom & Gwen Paton—Seymour House Bed & Breakfast,
South Haven

6 cups WATER
6 fresh PEACHES, sliced
POWDERED SUGAR

3/4 cup VANILLA YOGURT
1 cup fresh BLUEBERRIES
6 MINT LEAVES

Heat 6 cups of water to boiling and turn off heat. Place peaches in water until skin color fades. Immediately run under cold water and peel off skin. Sprinkle whole peaches with a fruit protector to keep from browning. Place in a covered container and chill for an hour. When ready to serve, slice peaches. Sprinkle powdered sugar on 7- or 8-inch clear glass plate and spread 2 tablespoons of yogurt on plate to within 1 inch of edge. Fan peach slices around the edge of each plate, mound blueberries in the center and garnish with a mint leaf.

Serves 6.

Applesauce & Cinnamon Parfait

"We like to make our own applesauce with locally grown Gala apples and fresh fruit, we also use flavored applesauce from the store for this recipe. We serve this as a breakfast fruit dish, with blueberry pancakes or corn-apple hotcakes."

John Hewett—Village Park Bed & Breakfast, Fruitport

1 jar (24 oz.) cranberry- or rhubarb-flavored APPLESAUCE
CINNAMON
1/4 cup chopped PECANS
1 jar (24 oz.) regular APPLESAUCE
1/2 cup finely diced APPLES
1 jar (24 oz.) raspberry-flavored APPLESAUCE
4 MARASCHINO CHERRIES

In parfait glasses or goblets, layer cranberry- or rhubarb-flavored applesauce followed by a layer of cinnamon and a layer of pecans. Use regular applesauce as the next layer, followed by another sprinkled layer of cinnamon and a thin layer of the finely diced apples. Layer apples with raspberry-flavored applesauce and sprinkle top with cinnamon. Garnish with a maraschino cherry.

Variation: Add a layer of granola or try other flavors of applesauce.

Serves 4.

Fruitport

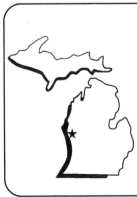

The Grand Haven and Muskegon area became famous in the late 1800s for its mineral springs. Great Lakes steamers brought health-conscious vacationers to visit a luxurious hotel with mineral baths. In the early 1900s, a pavilion was built which became the dance music and big band center of Michigan.

Cherry Rhubarb Crème Brûlée

"I serve this for breakfast with savory waffles or potato napoleons."

Janet Meteer—Bridgewalk Bed & Breakfast, Central Lake

2 Tbsp. unsalted BUTTER
1 cup RHUBARB, finely diced
1/2 cup SUGAR
1/4 cup GRENADINE or CHERRY LIQUEUR
2 cups WHIPPING CREAM
1/2 cup HALF & HALF
10 EGG YOLKS
2 tsp. VANILLA
1 cup fresh sweet CHERRIES, pitted and halved, or 1/2 cup dried
  TART CHERRIES
SUGAR for the top

Preheat oven to 300°. In a medium nonstick saucepan, heat butter over high heat. Add rhubarb, cooking until tender, about 5 minutes. Add sugar and grenadine or liqueur, cooking until sugar syrup is slightly caramelized. Add the creams, mixing to combine. Remove mixture from heat. In a large bowl, whisk egg yolks with vanilla. Slowly add rhubarb/cream mixture, stirring to combine. Divide cherries among 8 (4-oz.) ramekins. Spoon cream mixture over cherries. Place ramekins in pan filled with boiling water about 2/3 of the way up the sides. Place on lower rack of oven. Cook until lightly tan on top and a skewer inserted in center is hot to the touch, about 15-20 minutes. Remove to cake rack to cool. Cover and refrigerate overnight. To serve, preheat broiler. Evenly spread sugar over tops. Place under broiler to caramelize. Watch carefully. Cool 5 minutes, garnish with **MINT LEAVES** or **CHERRIES**

Serves 8.

Did you know?

Nearly 80 percent of the nation's red tart cherries are grown in Michigan.

SOUPS
&
SALADS

Summer Strawberry Soup

Flo Schermerhorn—Victorian 1898 Bed & Breakfast, Traverse City

3 cups APPLE JUICE or CIDER
3/4 cup plain YOGURT
3/4 cup WHIPPING CREAM
3 cups thinly sliced STRAWBERRIES
Additional YOGURT and MINT for garnish

Place juice in a chilled mixing bowl. Whisk in yogurt and cream until well combined. Stir in strawberries. Cover and refrigerate until ready to serve. To serve, garnish with a dollop of plain yogurt and a sprig of mint.

Serves 4.

Pauline's Low-Fat Chili

"I usually use a two-piece slow cooker and cook everything in the upper portion. That way, I don't have to wash two or more pans."

Pauline E. Spray—Lapeer

2 cups chopped ONIONS
2 cups chopped CELERY
3/4 lb. GROUND SIRLOIN
1 can (26 oz.) TOMATO SOUP
2 1/2 cups WATER
1 can (15.5 oz.) RED BEANS, drained
1 can (15.5 oz.) KIDNEY BEANS, drained
1 can (15.5 oz.) CHILI BEANS, undrained
1 rounded tsp. CHILI POWDER
1/4 tsp. CAYENNE PEPPER
SALT to taste

In a heavy pan or skillet, brown the onions, celery and ground sirloin. To this mixture, add the soup, beans and spices and simmer slowly for at least 2 hours.

Serves 6.

Taco Soup

"My family loves tacos so I created this recipe for a soup using their favorite ingredients."

Pat Bannick—Bannick's Bed & Breakfast, Diamondale

1 1/2 lbs. GROUND BEEF
1 lg. ONION, chopped
1 qt. diced TOMATOES, with juice
1 can (15 oz.) KIDNEY BEANS
1 can (15.25 oz.) WHOLE KERNEL CORN, with liquid
1 can (8 oz.) TOMATO SAUCE
1 pkg. TACO SEASONING MIX
3 cups WATER

In a Dutch oven, brown beef and onion. Drain fat and add remaining ingredients. Simmer for an hour. Serve with tortilla chips or corn bread.

Serves 8.

Mashed Potato Soup

"A chef at the Lansing capitol building used to make a bean soup that was similar to this. I didn't like beans, but love potatoes so I modified it to suit my tastes."

Joan M. Brown—Flint

6 cups cubed POTATOES
2 stalks CELERY, sliced
2 CARROTS, sliced
2 med. ONIONS, quartered and sliced
1 can (14.5 oz.) CHICKEN BROTH
WATER

1/8 cup minced PARSLEY
1 tsp. GARLIC SALT
1/4 tsp. PEPPER
1 Tbsp. BUTTER
1/4 cup MILK

Place 4 cups of the cubed potatoes in large pot. Add celery, carrots, onions and chicken broth. Add enough water to cover vegetables by about 2 inches. Season with parsley, garlic salt and pepper. Bring to a boil. Reduce heat. Cover and simmer at least 1 hour. Boil remaining 2 cups of potatoes for 20 minutes. Mash with butter and milk. Set aside. The last 10 minutes before serving soup, add the mashed potatoes. They will serve as the thickener for the soup. Simmer 10 minutes more.

Serves 6.

Flint

The vast white pine forests nearby attracted lumbermen to this area in the mid-1800s. Flint was incorporated as a city in 1855. By 1900, Flint's factories were making over 100,000 wooden road carts and carriages a year, and it became known as the "Vehicle City." General Motors was founded in Flint in 1908. Visit the 4,540 acre Genesee Recreation Area and Stepping Stone Falls, the spillway of the dam that impounds Mott Lake.

Lakeview Hill's White Chili

Lakeview Hills Resort and Croquet Club—Lewiston

2 lbs. boneless CHICKEN BREASTS
1 Tbsp. OLIVE OIL
2 med. ONIONS, chopped
4 cloves GARLIC, minced
2 cans (4 oz. ea.) mild GREEN CHILES, chopped
2 tsp. ground CUMIN
1 tsp. dried OREGANO, crumbled
1/4 tsp. ground CLOVES
1/4 tsp. CAYENNE PEPPER
2 cans (19 oz. ea.) CANNELLINI BEANS, drained
6 cups CHICKEN STOCK or CANNED BROTH
3 cups grated MONTEREY JACK CHEESE
SALT and PEPPER to taste
SOUR CREAM
fresh CILANTRO, chopped
SALSA

Place chicken in large, heavy saucepan. Add cold water to cover and bring to a simmer. Cook until just tender, about 15 minutes. Drain and cool. Remove skin and cut meat into cubes. In the same saucepan, heat the oil over medium-high heat. Add onions and sauté until translucent. Stir in garlic, then chiles, cumin, oregano, cloves and cayenne and sauté for 2 minutes. Add beans and stock and bring to a boil. Reduce heat and simmer until beans are tender, stirring occasionally (about 30 minutes).* Add chicken and 1 cup cheese to chili and stir until cheese melts. Season to taste with salt and pepper. Ladle chili into bowls. Divide remaining cheese among serving bowls and add dollops of sour cream to each. Garnish with cilantro. Serve with salsa on the side.

Serves 8-10.

*Cover and refrigerate at this point if you plan to serve the following day. When ready to finish preparation, place bean mixture in a large heavy saucepan and bring to a simmer. Continue as per instructions above.

Swiss Onion Soup

"This soup makes a fine base for creamy pasta sauces, and may be stored, frozen, for 2-3 months."

John E. Sisson—Leelanau Country Inn, Maple City

2 cups WATER
5 Tbsp. BUTTER
1 tsp. GARLIC PURÉE
3 cups thinly sliced ONION
3/4 tsp. DRY MUSTARD
1/2 tsp. SALT
1 1/2 cups MILK
3 Tbsp. FLOUR
1 1/2 cups shredded SWISS CHEESE
1/2 tsp. PREPARED HORSERADISH
1 Tbsp. DRY SHERRY
1/2 Tbsp. GROUND BLACK PEPPER
1/2 tsp. SOY SAUCE
3 drops TABASCO® SAUCE
2 shakes WORCESTERSHIRE SAUCE

In a saucepan, combine water, 2 tablespoons butter, garlic purée, onion slices, mustard and salt; cover and simmer over low heat, until onions are tender (about 20 minutes). Scald milk. In separate saucepan, make a roux by melting remaining 3 tablespoons butter and blending in flour; stir while cooking over low heat for 5 minutes. Add scalded milk to roux, mixing well to make a medium-thick cream sauce. (Scalded milk must be hot when added to the roux, to make cream sauce thicken quickly.) Slowly add shredded cheese to sauce, mixing until melted.   Add horseradish and sherry to cheese sauce and combine the cheese sauce with contents of saucepan containing onions, mixing thoroughly. Mix in pepper, soy, Tabasco and Worcestershire sauce.

Makes 5 cups of soup.

Erwtensoep
(Dutch Pea Soup)

"From the Holland Junior Welfare League's cookbook Eet Smakelijk, *which is a Dutch phrase that means 'eat well and with taste.'"*

Courtesy Wendy Link—Holland Area Convention & Visitors Bureau, Holland

1 lb. dried PEAS
1 med. PIG HOCK, SHOULDER
   PORK or METWORST
3 qts. WATER
SALT and PEPPER to taste
1 1/2 cups diced CELERY

3 med. ONIONS, chopped
3 POTATOES, diced
2 CARROTS, diced
PARSLEY, to taste
1 cup MILK

Soak peas overnight completely covered with cold water. Drain. In a saucepan, combine meat, peas and water and simmer for 2 hours. Add next 5 ingredients and cook for 1 hour. Add parsley and milk and continue cooking for 10 minutes.

Serves 8-10.

Chicken Salad Deluxe

"I serve this salad with strips of watermelon, cantaloupe, honeydew melon and hot croissants. Everyone loves it!

Mary Jo Henrickson—Elmhurst Bed & Breakfast, Shelby

1 cup seedless GREEN GRAPES
1 1/2 cups cubed CELERY
1 1/2 cups cooked, cubed CHICKEN
1 cup MAYONNAISE
1 1/2 cups dry CHINESE NOODLES
1/2 cup whole SMOKED, ROASTED ALMONDS
CURLY ENDIVE

In a bowl, combine and mix grapes, celery, chicken and mayonnaise. Refrigerate. When ready to serve, add noodles and almonds and toss chicken mixture gently. Place mixture in a serving dish lined with the curly endive.

Serves 6.

Sirloin Salad

"This recipe by Cynthia P. Hodges, Ann Arbor, was one of the 15 entries from the Michigan Beef Cookoff contests to compete in the National Beef Cookoff."

Courtesy Michigan Beef Industry Commission, Okemos

2 TOP SIRLOIN STEAKS, cut 1-inch thick
Marinade:
   2 tsp. minced GARLIC
   1 tsp. SALT
   1/2 tsp. BLACK PEPPER
   1/2 cup RED WINE VINEGAR
   1 cup OLIVE OIL
4 heads BOSTON LETTUCE, washed and cored
8 oz. BLUE CHEESE, crumbled
1 cup dried CHERRIES
1 cup PIGNOLI (pine nuts)

Cut steaks lengthwise in half, then crosswise into 1/8-inch-thick strips. Combine marinade mixture ingredients in a small bowl. Place half of marinade in a shallow dish, add steak slices and marinate for 30 minutes. Carefully separate several large lettuce leaves and arrange on 4 plates. Tear remaining lettuce into bite-size pieces and toss with the balance of the marinade mixture until coated. Stir-fry beef over medium-high heat for 1 to 2 minutes or until cooked to taste. Arrange beef strips on lettuce and sprinkle with blue cheese, cherries and pignoli.

Serves 4.

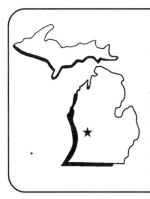

Grand Rapids

Named for the Grand River rapids, Grand Rapids began as a trading post in 1826. This city is renowned as a producer of quality furniture. Don't miss one of America's top road races, the Old Kent River Bank Run in May; Festival in June; and the Celebration on the Grand in September.

Snicker Salad

"Comfort is served 'homestyle' at our bed and breakfast. We are located on 50 acres of rolling hillside that includes 2 ponds. Jacuzzi suites and many more amenities, including a bicycle built for two, await our guests."

Lyn Gross—Country View Bed & Breakfast, Marlette

2 GRANNY SMITH APPLES
2 RED DELICIOUS APPLES
6 SNICKERS® CANDY BARS, cubed
1 tub (8 oz.) COOL WHIP®

Wash, core and cube apples. Combine apples and candy, add Cool Whip and toss.

Serves 6-10.

Stuffed Tomatoes

"This is a great recipe for entertaining. I serve it often when I have luncheon guests."

Tina Rivera, Saginaw

6 med. TOMATOES
2 boiled EGGS, chopped
1/2 cup chopped CELERY
1/2 cup chopped CUCUMBER
1 Tbsp. diced ONION
1/4 cup chopped GREEN BELL PEPPER
2 Tbsp. MAYONNAISE
SALT and PEPPER to taste
1/4 cup slivered ALMONDS
SOUR CREAM

Remove tops of tomatoes and scoop out centers, leaving shells that are 1/4-inch thick. Turn upside down to drain. Dice tomato pulp and combine with remaining ingredients. Stuff tomatoes, top with a dollop of sour cream and serve on a bed of lettuce leaves.

Serves 6.

Holiday Potato Salad

Catherine Mattingly—Vicksburg

4 cups cooked, diced POTATOES
3 hard-boiled EGGS, chopped
1 cup diced CELERY
1/4 cup diced GREEN ONIONS
1/4 cup PIMENTOS
1/4 cup diced GREEN BELL
   PEPPERS
1/4 cup chopped PARSLEY
1/2 tsp. SALT

1 cup MAYONNAISE
1/2 cup WHIPPED CREAM
1 envelope KNOX® GELATIN
1/4 cup COLD WATER
1 cup BOILING WATER
1/4 cup LEMON JUICE
2 Tbsp. SUGAR
1 tsp. SALT
STUFFED GREEN OLIVES

In a large bowl, combine first 10 ingredients. In a small bowl, combine gelatin and cold water. When gelatin has softened, add boiling water, lemon juice, sugar and salt. Pour a thin layer of gelatin mixture into a 10-inch tube mold. Let stand until firm. Fold the remaining gelatin mixture into potato mixture and ladle into mold on top of gelatin. Garnish with olives. Store, covered, in refrigerator until ready to serve.

Serves 8.

Pansy's Cole Slaw

Pansy Goble—Jackson

1 head CABBAGE, shredded
1 med. ONION, chopped
1 GREEN BELL PEPPER, diced
1/2 cup VEGETABLE OIL
1 cup VINEGAR
1 1/2 cups SUGAR
1 Tbsp. SALT

Combine cabbage, onion and pepper in a large bowl. Place oil, vinegar, sugar and salt in a saucepan and bring to a boil. Pour over cabbage mixture. Cover to keep steam in. Let stand several hours. Stir and refrigerate.

Serves 8.

Marinated 3-Bean Salad

"This was my mother, Bernice Chewning's, recipe."

Barbara Barnes—Hanover

1 can (16 oz.) cut GREEN BEANS
1 can (16 oz.) cut WAX BEANS
1 can (16 oz.) KIDNEY BEANS
1/2 cup chopped GREEN BELL PEPPER
3/4 cup SUGAR
1/3 cup SALAD OIL
2/3 cup VINEGAR
SALT and PEPPER to taste

Drain beans and combine in a large glass bowl. Stir in bell pepper. In another bowl, combine the sugar, oil and vinegar. Pour sugar mixture over bean mixture. Add salt and pepper and toss all together. Chill overnight. Before serving, toss again to coat beans with marinade. Drain excess liquids before serving.

Serves 6-8

Layered Salad

"My daughter gave me this recipe. It's a perfect salad for Sunday dinner because it can be made the night before."

Anna Hubbell—Reading

1/2 head LETTUCE
1 layer ONION, chopped
1 layer CELERY, chopped
1 can sliced WATER
    CHESTNUTS, drained
1 pkg. (10 oz.) frozen PEAS,
    thawed
1 1/2 cups MAYONNAISE
2 Tbsp. SUGAR
BACON BITS, as desired

In a large glass or ceramic bowl, layer lettuce, onion, celery water chestnuts and peas in order given. In a small bowl, combine the mayonnaise, sugar and bacon bits. Spread mayonnaise mixture over top of peas. Cover with plastic wrap and refrigerate overnight. Stir together just before serving.

Serves 8-10.

Shirley's Cole Slaw

Shirley Densmore—Jackson

2 qts. shredded CABBAGE
2 GREEN BELL PEPPERS, chopped
1 RED BELL PEPPER or PIMENTO, chopped
4 med. ONIONS, diced
Dressing:
   1 pt. VINEGAR
   1 tsp. CELERY SEED
   1/2 tsp. TURMERIC
   1 1/2 tsp. SALT
   1 1/2 tsp. MUSTARD SEED
   2 1/2 cups SUGAR

Combine salad ingredients in a large bowl. In a saucepan, combine dressing ingredients and bring to a boil. While dressing is still hot, pour over salad ingredients. Let stand, covered, in refrigerator at least 24 hours before serving.

Serves 8.

Lettuce Salad

Ellen Colburn—Brooklyn

1 med. head LETTUCE, cut up
6 to 8 hard-boiled EGGS, chopped
1/2 to 3/4 cup diced CHEDDAR CHEESE
1 can (15 oz.) tiny SWEET PEAS, drained
1 ONION, diced
1/2 cup chopped CELERY
1/2 to 3/4 cup SWEET BREAD & BUTTER PICKLES, halved

Dressing:
   4 Tbsp. SUGAR   4 Tbsp. VINEGAR
   4 Tbsp. (heaping) SALAD   4 Tbsp. CREAM
      DRESSING   SALT to taste

Combine salad ingredients in a large bowl. In a small bowl, combine dressing ingredients. Add dressing to salad and toss before serving.

Serves 6.

Poppy Seed Pasta Salad

"These are the vegetables we use at the Inn; however, any fresh vegetables you may prefer will work as well. Adding a drained can of dark red kidney beans is a nice touch."

John E. Sisson—Leelanau Country Inn, Maple City

1 lb. COOKED PASTA, (shells, spirals, elbows, etc.)
1 med. RED ONION, diced
2 med. GREEN BELL PEPPERS, diced
2 med. TOMATOES, diced
1 lg. CUCUMBER, peeled, diced
1 cup CELERY, diced
1/2 lb. fresh PEA PODS, blanched
2 cups grated PARMESAN CHEESE
2 Tbsp. POPPY SEEDS
2 cups GREEK DRESSING (see below)

Prepare pasta according to package directions, drain and rinse under cold running water. In large mixing bowl, combine pasta with remaining ingredients. Mix well and chill before serving.

Serves 8.

Note: This salad can be stored, sealed, in the refrigerator for up to four days.

Greek Dressing

2 cups CANOLA OIL
3/4 cup APPLE CIDER VINEGAR
1/2 Tbsp. SUGAR
1/2 Tbsp. SALT
1/4 tsp. minced BASIL LEAF
1/8 tsp. ground WHITE PEPPER
1/2 Tbsp. dried OREGANO
3/4 Tbsp. GARLIC PURÉE

In a glass bowl, mix all ingredients together well. It is always best to make dressings at least a day ahead of use, to allow the flavors to blend. This dressing can be stored, sealed and refrigerated for up to one month.

Yields 3 cups.

MAIN DISHES

Pat's Chicken Divan

Pat Hollis—Allen Park

1 (2 1/2-3 lb.) cooked CHICKEN, deboned, skin removed, cubed
2 pkgs. (10 oz. ea.) frozen BROCCOLI, thawed
1 can (10.75 oz.) CREAM OF CHICKEN SOUP
1/3 cup MAYONNAISE
1 tsp. LEMON JUICE
1/3 tsp. CURRY POWDER
1/2 cup grated SHARP CHEDDAR CHEESE
1 pkg. (16 oz.) PEPPERIDGE FARM® HERB DRESSING

Preheat oven to 250°. Layer chicken and broccoli in an oiled 9 x 13 baking pan. Combine soup, mayonnaise, lemon juice and curry powder. Pour soup mixture over chicken and broccoli. Sprinkle with cheese and top with herb dressing. Bake for 45 minutes.

Serves 6.

Saucijzenbroodjes

(Pig in the Blankets)

"Saucijzenbroodjes are made in mass quantities by church groups and sold for fund raisers."

Mary Jo Wiswedel—Holland Area Convention & Visitors Bureau, Holland

1 1/2 lbs. GROUND PORK
1 1/2 lbs. GROUND BEEF
2 EGGS
1/3 cup MILK
3/4 cup crushed RUSK* or SALTINE CRACKERS
1/2 tsp. NUTMEG
4 1/2 cups FLOUR
1 Tbsp. BAKING POWDER
1 1/2 tsp. SALT
3 sticks OLEO or BUTTER
2 EGGS
1 1/3 cups MILK

Mix pork and beef. Lightly beat eggs and mix with milk. Add cracker crumbs and nutmeg and combine. Add to meat mixture and mix well. Form meat mixture into link sausage shapes. Sift together the flour, baking powder and salt. Cut in margarine as for pie dough. Mix eggs and milk together and add to dry mixture. Knead lightly and form into a smooth ball. Roll dough to 1/4-inch thickness, cut into 3 1/2-inch squares. Place meat "sausages" in center. Wrap loosely in dough, overlapping on the bottom. Do not pinch ends shut. Place on an ungreased baking sheet and bake at 375° for 30 minutes or until golden brown. Serve with ketchup or maple syrup on the side.

Makes 30 to 36 "Pigs."

*Rusk is a thick, cracker-type product available in local grocery stores or may be found in gourmet food shops.

Swedish Meatball Dinner

Barbara Bartman—Jackson

1 cup BREAD CRUMBS
1 EGG, beaten
1/2 cup MILK
1 lb. GROUND BEEF
1/2 tsp. dry MUSTARD
1/2 tsp. CELERY SALT
1/4 tsp. NUTMEG
3 Tbsp. grated ONION

FLOUR
2 Tbsp. BACON DRIPPINGS
1 can (10.75 oz.) CREAM OF
  MUSHROOM SOUP
3/4 cup MILK
2 1/2 - 3 cups cooked
  VEGETABLES, drained
SALT and PEPPER to taste

Place bread crumbs in a large bowl, combine egg and milk and pour over crumbs. Add meat, mustard, celery salt, nutmeg and onion and combine well. Shape into small balls. Roll each ball lightly in flour. In a skillet, add bacon drippings and meatballs. Cook slowly, turning frequently, until meatballs are browned, about 20 minutes. Remove meatballs from skillet and keep warm while making gravy. Add soup and milk to drippings in skillet, cooking and stirring until smooth. Stir in vegetables and add salt and pepper to taste. Return meatballs to skillet and heat through.

Serves 4-6.

Mrs. Surratt's Meat Loaf

"The boiled eggs are very attractive when you slice the meat loaf, and they make cold meat loaf sandwiches even better!"

Mrs. R. L. Suratt—Charlevoix

2 lbs. GROUND ROUND
1 lb. GROUND PORK
2 tsp. SAGE
1 ONION, chopped
2 EGGS, beaten

SALT and PEPPER to taste
1 cup MILK
14-15 CRACKERS, crushed
3-4 HARD-BOILED EGGS

Preheat oven to 450°. Combine all ingredients except eggs, form into a loaf and place in loaf pan. Push hard-boiled eggs in a row down the center. Bake for 45 minutes.

Serves 6.

Chicken with Grapefruit

"A little something different. This dish can be made in half an hour, give or take a few minutes."

Mollie Rogers—Chimney Corners, Crystal Lake

1 cup FLOUR
SALT and PEPPER to taste
2 1/2-3 lbs. CHICKEN pieces
3 Tbsp. BUTTER
3 Tbsp. OIL
3/4 cup CHICKEN BROTH or STOCK
1/3 cup dry WHITE WINE
1 Tbsp. dry SHERRY, MADEIRA or BRANDY
1 GRAPEFRUIT, peeled, sectioned, juice squeezed and reserved
1 Tbsp. BUTTER

Combine flour, salt and pepper and dredge chicken pieces in flour mixture. Heat butter and oil in a large skillet and fry chicken, uncovered, over fairly high heat, turning pieces so that they brown evenly on all sides. Cook about 20 minutes, or until chicken is tender. Transfer cooked chicken to a warm platter. Add chicken broth, wine and your choice of sherry, madeira, or brandy to the skillet, then add the grapefruit juice. Stir well, loosening up all the brown bits. Boil liquid down to about half its original quantity. When sauce has thickened a bit, stir in butter and add grapefruit sections. Place chicken in a large serving dish; pour sauce over top. Serve with ***Rosemary Roasters***.

Serves 6.

Rosemary Roasters

Mollie Rogers—Chimney Corners, Crystal Lake

Unpeeled sm. RED POTATOES or WHITE "BOILERS,"
   sliced lengthwise
OLIVE OIL
dried ROSEMARY

Wash potatoes and roll in olive oil. Sprinkle rosemary with a fairly lavish hand. Place in a baking dish and roast at 350° for about 30 minutes or until tender and lightly browned.

Substitute Crab Quiche

"This dish is great for any meal!"

Barbara Inwood—Woods Inn, Ann Arbor

1/2 cup MAYONNAISE
2 Tbsp. FLOUR
1 pkg. CRAB SUBSTITUTE
1/3 GREEN ONION

1 Tbsp. PARSLEY
2 cups SWISS CHEESE
1 unbaked PASTRY SHELL

Preheat oven to 350°. Combine all ingredients thoroughly and place in the pie shell. Bake for 1 hour.

Serves 6-8.

Ann Arbor

Surrounded by villages and farm-lands, Ann Arbor is the home of the University of Michigan. Here you can find a year-round calendar of festivals and fairs. The city's concerts, theater, dance, movies, special events and museums draw visitors from across the state and indeed the country. Nearby rivers, lakes and recreation areas attract sports enthusiasts throughout the year.

Swiss Steak

Catherine Mattingly—Vicksburg

1 SIRLOIN or ROUND STEAK
2 1/2 cups TOMATO JUICE
1 ONION, sliced

SALT and PEPPER to taste
1 can (4.5 oz.) sliced
MUSHROOMS

Preheat oven to 350°. Place steak in a casserole dish. Add tomato juice, onion, salt and pepper. Cover, and bake for 2 1/2 hours. Twenty minutes before done, add mushrooms. Remove meat from skillet and make gravy with the drippings.

Serves 4-6.

American Fluff

Theresa A. Grupa—Charlevoix

3 Tbsp. BUTTER
1 lg. ONION, finely chopped
1 1/2 lbs. GROUND BEEF
SALT and PEPPER to taste
1 can (15 oz.) GREEN PEAS, drained
1 can (4.5 oz.) MUSHROOMS, drained
1/2 cup CELERY, chopped
1/4 cup chopped GREEN BELL PEPPER
2 cans (10.75 oz. ea.) TOMATO SOUP
1 cup cooked RICE
4-5 strips uncooked BACON

Preheat oven to 350°. In a skillet, melt butter and add onion, meat, salt and pepper. Sauté until onions are translucent. Add and combine remaining ingredients (except bacon). Place mixture in a buttered casserole dish and lay strips of bacon over top. Bake for 1 hour.

Serves 4-6

Open-Face Corned Beef Treats

"This makes a good dish for either breakfast or lunch."

Joyce A. Runberg—Beaver Island

1 can (12 oz.) CORNED BEEF, crumbled
1 1/2 cups shredded CHEESE (1/2 white; 1/2 sharp yellow)
3 Tbsp. MAYONNAISE
1/3 cup SOUR CREAM
1/3 GREEN BELL PEPPER, chopped
3 GREEN ONIONS, chopped
DILL WEED and GARLIC POWDER, to taste
6 ENGLISH MUFFINS

Combine all ingredients, except muffins, and mix thoroughly. Spread mixture on split English muffins. Place in a toaster oven or broiler and broil until golden brown and bubbly.

Serves 6.

Pecan Whitefish
with Compound Butter

"This dish is especially terrific if served with grilled asparagus and rice."

Kate & Barbara Vilter—The Riverside Inn (Chef Thomas Sawyer), Leland

6-8 (8 oz. ea.) WHITEFISH FILLETS
1/2 cups DRY WHITE WINE
1/4 cup OLIVE OIL
2 cups crushed PECANS

Place fillets on broiler pan. Drizzle wine and oil over fillets, and then coat with crushed pecans. Broil for approximately 6 minutes, or until wine and oil are bubbling. Add 2 slices of *Compound Butter* to each fillet, and continue broiling for about a minute or until butter has begun to melt. Remove and serve immediately.

Serves 6-8.

Compound Butter with Cherries

1 cup dried CHERRIES
1/4 cup WATER
juice of 1/4 fresh GRAPEFRUIT
juice of 1/4 fresh LIME
juice of 1/2 fresh ORANGE
2 tsp. ORANGE ZEST
1 lb. BUTTER (at room temperature)

Reconstitute dried cherries with 1/4 cup water by simmering them over low heat until cherries are soft. Do not discard water. Blend cherries, water from reconstitution, juices and zest together in a blender until smooth, adding additional water if necessary. Spread room temperature butter out evenly on waxed paper to about a 1/4-inch thickness. Chill butter until firm. Spread cherry mixture evenly over chilled butter. Then, you can either roll butter into a log by using waxed paper as a guide, or you can cut butter into small serving size triangles. Compound butter can be frozen for approximately 3 weeks. Slice as needed.

Applesauce Meatballs

"I was given this recipe by my mother-in-law many years ago and it has been a family favorite ever since."

Odula Reed—Okapi Inn, New Era

1 lb. GROUND BEEF
1/2 cup APPLESAUCE
1 EGG
1 med. ONION, diced
6 slices BREAD, crumbled
1/2 cup FLOUR

OIL
SALT and PEPPER to taste
1 GREEN BELL PEPPER cut
   into thin slices
1 can (8 oz.) TOMATO SAUCE

Combine first 5 ingredients in a mixing bowl. Mix well. Place flour in a shallow dish. Form meat mixture into 1 inch balls, roll in flour and brown in skillet to which oil has been added. Preheat oven to 350°. Using a slotted spoon, place browned meatballs in a casserole dish. Sprinkle with salt and pepper to taste and layer with bell pepper slices. Drizzle tomato sauce over all. Cover and bake 40 minutes.

Serves 6.

Detroit

Antoine de la Mothe Cadillac, a French colonist, founded Detroit in 1701. Known as the "Automobile Capital of the World" or "Motor City," Detroit is Michigan's largest city, and is the sixth largest in the U.S. In the early 1900s, Henry T. Ford's Model T started an automobile manufacturing boom that continues to this day. Detroit is one of the world's busiest inland ports, a great steel center and leader in the manufacture of many products such as pharmaceuticals, office equipment, paint and rubber products. More than half of the garden seed used throughout the country comes from this city.

Turkey Hot Dog Casserole

Artha Neuenfeldt—Jackson

1 pkg. frozen TATER TOTS or HASH BROWNS, thawed
3 or 4 TURKEY HOT DOGS, sliced in small rounds
1 tsp. MUSTARD
1 Tbsp. BROWN SUGAR
1 can (16 oz.) diced TOMATOES, drained
1/4 cup chopped ONIONS
6 slices AMERICAN CHEESE

Preheat oven to 350°. Arrange potatoes in bottom of an oiled casserole dish and layer with hot dog slices. Combine mustard and brown sugar with tomatoes and layer over meat. Sprinkle top with onions. Bake 25 minutes. Arrange cheese over top of casserole and bake another 5 minutes or until cheese melts.

Serves 4.

Mexicorn Bake

Anna Hubbell—Reading

1 lb. lean GROUND BEEF
1 med. GREEN BELL PEPPER, chopped
1/2 pkg. TACO SEASONING
3/4 cup WATER
1 can (10.75 oz.) GOLDEN CORN SOUP
1/4 cup MILK
1 pkg. (10 oz.) refrigerated BISCUITS
1/2 cup shredded CHEDDAR CHEESE

Preheat oven to 400°. In large skillet over medium high heat cook beef and bell pepper until beef is browned, stirring to separate meat. Drain off fat. Add taco seasoning and water. Simmer 5 minutes. Stir in soup and milk. Pour mixture into an oiled 2- to 3-quart casserole or baking dish. Bake 10 minutes or until mixture begins to bubble. Remove dish from oven; stir. Separate biscuits; cut each in half. Place biscuits, cut side down, over hot meat mixture in spoke wheel design around edge of casserole. Sprinkle cheese over biscuits. Bake 15 minutes or until biscuits are golden brown.

Serves 6.

Chicken & Spinach Lasagna

Faith Apol—Caledonia

1/2 cup MARGARINE or BUTTER
2 cloves GARLIC, minced
1/2 cup FLOUR
1 tsp. SALT
2 cups MILK
2 cups CHICKEN BROTH
1 med. ONION
1/2 tsp. dried BASIL
1/2 tsp. dried OREGANO
1/4 tsp. PEPPER
2 cups shredded MOZZARELLA CHEESE
1 cup grated PARMESAN CHEESE, divided
9 (8 oz.) uncooked LASAGNA NOODLES
1 ctn. (16 oz.) small curd COTTAGE CHEESE
2 cups cooked, diced CHICKEN
2 pkgs. (10 oz. ea.) frozen CHOPPED SPINACH, thawed
    and well drained

Heat margarine over low heat until melted. Add garlic, flour and salt. Cook, stirring constantly, until bubbly. Remove from heat, stir in milk and broth and heat to boiling, stirring constantly. Boil and stir 1 minute. Stir in the onion, basil, oregano, pepper, mozzarella, and half of the Parmesan cheese. Cook over low heat, stirring constantly, until mozzarella is melted. Preheat oven to 350°. Spread 1/4 of cheese sauce (about 1 1/2 cups) in an ungreased 9 x 13 baking dish. Top with 3 uncooked noodles. Spread half of cottage cheese over noodles. Top with 1/4 of cheese sauce, 3 noodles and remaining cottage cheese. Sprinkle chicken evenly over cheese. Add spinach, 1/4 of cheese sauce, remaining noodles and remaining cheese sauce. Top with the remaining Parmesan cheese. Bake, uncovered for 35-40 minutes, or until noodles are cooked. Let stand 15 minutes before cutting.

Serves 9-12.

Pesto Beef Sandwich in-the-Round

"This recipe, by Patti Dietlin of Kewadin, was one of the 15 entries from the Michigan Beef Cookoff contests to compete in the National Beef Cookoff."

Courtesy Michigan Beef Industry Commission, Okemos

1 (12-inch) round, whole BREAD LOAF
1/3 cup LIGHT MAYONNAISE
3 Tbsp. prepared PESTO SAUCE
1 tsp. fresh LEMON JUICE
1 lb. rare ROAST BEEF, thinly sliced
1 jar (7 oz.) roasted RED PEPPERS,* drained
4 oz. mixed SALAD GREENS
4 oz. FETA or GOAT CHEESE, crumbled
BLACK PEPPER

Slice bread loaf in half lengthwise and remove center, leaving a 1-inch shell. In a small bowl, combine mayonnaise, pesto sauce and lemon juice. Spread mixture on both halves of the bread. Layer roast beef, roasted red peppers, salad greens and cheese on one half of loaf, top with second half and cut into 5 wedges. Serve immediately or wrap in foil or plastic wrap and refrigerate until ready to serve.

Serves 5.

*1 jar (4 oz.) chopped pimentos may be substituted for the red peppers.

Battle Creek

An abolitionist stronghold before the Civil War, Battle Creek became the home of ex-slave Sojourner Truth who was famous for her crusade for truth and freedom. Known as the breakfast food center of the nation, Battle Creek is home to the Kellogg Co., the Post division of Kraft-General Foods Corp., and the Ralston Purina Co.

Hamburger Patty Casserole

"This is a great favorite for pot-luck suppers ."

Terri Jaskerski—Charlevoix

1 lb. GROUND BEEF
1 EGG
1/2 cup BREAD CRUMBS
1 sm. ONION, grated
6 slices BREAD, cubed
1 ONION, chopped

4 Tbsp. BUTTER, melted
1/4 tsp. SAGE
1 can (10.75 oz.) CREAM OF
  MUSHROOM SOUP
1/2 cup WATER

Preheat oven to 350°. Combine hamburger, egg, bread crumbs and grated onion. Form into small patties and brown in a skillet. Combine cubed bread, chopped onion, butter and sage. Layer patties and bread mixture in casserole dish. Combine soup and water and pour over all. Bake 30 minutes.

Serves 4.

Spicy Stuffed Peppers

"This recipe was created because I found all other stuffed pepper recipes to be bland. Pizza sauce already combined the flavor and consistency I wanted so I made it once, and have never altered anything else except to make bigger batches!"

Pat Akers-Goggans—The North House, a Victorian Respite, Vassar

1 lb. GROUND BEEF
1 stalk CELERY, chopped
1 small ONION, chopped
1 cup uncooked WHITE RICE
1 EGG
1 can (15 oz.) PIZZA SAUCE WITH CHEESE, divided
4 lg. GREEN BELL PEPPERS, tops removed, seeded

Preheat oven to 400°. Mix ground beef, celery, onion, rice, egg and 3/4 of the can of pizza sauce. Stuff peppers. Place peppers in a deep ovenproof dish or pan. Add water to remaining 1/4 can of sauce to make a full can. Pour sauce over top of peppers. Cover and bake for 1 hour and 45 minutes.

Serves 4.

Rosalyn's Gefilte Fish

"I made this recipe many times when my husband brought home fresh fish caught in Lake Michigan."

Rosalyn Goldstick, Charlevoix

5 lbs. mixed WHITEFISH and TROUT, filleted,
**   heads and tails reserved**
1 CARROT, sliced
2 ONIONS, quartered
WATER
1 3/4 cups chopped ONION
6 EGGS, lightly beaten
1 1/2 cups MATZOH MEAL
1 CARROT, finely ground
1 Tbsp. chopped PARSLEY
1 Tbsp. CELERY FLAKES
SALT and PEPPER to taste

Place heads and tails of fish in a large pot, add sliced carrot, quartered onions and enough water to cover. Place a layer of cheesecloth over the mixture. In a food processor, coarsely grind the filleted fish. In a large bowl, combine the ground fish, chopped onion, eggs, matzoh meal and ground carrot. Form fish mixture into balls (or oval cakes). Carefully lower balls into the fish broth. Simmer for 1 1/2 hours, shaking pan occasionally to prevent sticking. Place fish balls on a large platter to cool. Garnish each with a carrot slice. Strain broth and serve on the side or use to reheat. Serve gefilte fish warm or cold with horseradish on the side.

Lansing

Settlers first came to the site of Lansing in 1837, and it became the state capital in 1847. R. E. Olds built his first motor vehicles here and this city has gone on to become an important automotive center.

Tuna-Macaroni Loaf

Mary Louise Novotny, Charlevoix

1 can (12 oz.) EVAPORATED MILK
1/2 cup WATER
1 1/2 cups grated AMERICAN or CHEDDAR CHEESE
3 Tbsp. BUTTER
1 1/4 cups BREAD CRUMBS
1/4 cup finely chopped ONION
1/4 cup chopped PIMENTO
1 can (12 oz.) TUNA, drained
SALT and PEPPER to taste
3 cups cooked, drained MACARONI
3 EGGS, lightly beaten

Preheat oven to 350°. In a large saucepan, combine milk, water, cheese and butter and simmer until cheese has melted. Remove pan from heat and add the bread crumbs, onion, pimento, tuna, salt and pepper. Stir macaroni and lightly beaten eggs into tuna mixture. Place in a greased loaf pan and bake for 1 1/2 hours.

Serves 6-8.

Ham Croquettes

Mrs. Henry Partridge—Charlevoix

2 cups ground, cooked HAM
1/4 cup grated ONION
1 cup grated CARROTS
1 cup BREAD CRUMBS
1 EGG, well beaten
SALT and PEPPER to taste
1 can (10.75 oz.) CREAM OF CHICKEN SOUP
1 can (15 oz.) GREEN PEAS

Preheat oven to 350°. Mix first seven ingredients together well and shape into croquettes. Place croquettes on a greased cookie sheet and bake for 40 minutes. Just before serving, combine soup and peas in a saucepan and warm through. Serve over top of croquettes.

Stuffed Green Peppers

"This is my mother's recipe that I have adapted to suit my own tastes. I consider this a main course, but it can also be used as a side dish. When I make this dish, most of the ingredients come from my own garden."

Gilda Greenwood—Flint

4 lg. well-shaped GREEN BELL PEPPERS
1 cup RICE
3 med. TOMATOES, diced
1 med. ZUCCHINI, diced
1/2 pkg. frozen MIXED VEGETABLES, cooked and drained
1 med. ONION, diced
1 1/2 tsp. GARLIC POWDER
2 tsp. DILL WEED
1 Tbsp. dried BASIL
SALT and PEPPER to taste
1 Tbsp. CRAZY® SALT
1 lb. GROUND TURKEY, cooked and drained

Remove tops, core and seed peppers. Set aside. Cook rice according to package directions. Add remaining ingredients to rice and stir well. Spoon mixture into each of the peppers. For best flavor, refrigerate overnight. Bake at 375° for 45 minutes.

Serves 4.

Sault St. Marie

Sault Ste. Marie is the oldest town in Michigan, with a mission having been established here in 1668. Famous for its Soo Locks, through which millions of tons of cargo pass each year, this city is connected to its twin, Sault Ste. Marie, Canada, by the 2-mile-long International Bridge. The locks were created in 1885 to allow cargo ships to pass between Lakes Superior and Huron, thus avoiding the 21-foot drop and ensuing rapids between these two bodies of water.

Roast Pork
with Raspberry Sauce

This recipe and the front cover photo are courtesy of the National Pork Producers Council, Detroit.

1 (3-4 lb.) rolled BONELESS PORK LOIN ROAST
1 tsp. SALT
1 tsp. GROUND BLACK PEPPER
1 tsp. GROUND SAGE
RASPBERRY SAUCE
1 LEMON, sliced

Preheat oven to 325°. Sprinkle roast with salt, pepper and sage. Place on rack in shallow roasting pan; bake for 1 1/2-2 hours or until meat thermometer registers 160°. Place roast on serving platter and slice. Drizzle with a small amount of **Raspberry Sauce** and garnish with lemon slices.

Raspberry Sauce

1 pkg. (12 oz.) frozen RASPBERRIES, thawed
1 1/2 cups SUGAR
1/4 cup WHITE VINEGAR
1/4 tsp. GROUND CLOVES
1/4 tsp. GROUND GINGER
1/4 tsp. GROUND NUTMEG
1/4 cup CORNSTARCH
1 Tbsp. LEMON JUICE
1 Tbsp. BUTTER or MARGARINE, melted
3 to 4 drops RED FOOD COLORING

Drain raspberries; reserve liquid, adding water (if necessary) to make 3/4 cup. Combine 1/2 cup raspberry liquid with sugar, vinegar, cloves, ginger and nutmeg in a medium saucepan; bring to a boil. reduce heat; simmer, uncovered, for 10 minutes. Blend cornstarch and remaining 1/4 cup raspberry liquid; add to saucepan. Cook over medium heat, stirring constantly, 1 minute or until thickened. Stir in raspberries, lemon juice, butter and food coloring. Pour sauce into a serving dish and serve with roast pork.

SIDE DISHES

Butter Bean Casserole

Barbara Barnes—Hanover

2 cups cooked BUTTER BEANS
1 cup canned, diced TOMATOES
1 med. ONION, sliced
3/4 cup packed BROWN SUGAR
6 slices BACON
SALT and PEPPER to taste

Preheat oven to 350°. In a casserole dish, place beans, tomatoes, onion, brown sugar and bacon in layers in the order given. Season to taste. Bake for 1 hour.

Serves 4-6.

Stewed Tomatoes

"This may seem like a lot of work, when one could open a can of stewed tomatoes, heat and serve. However, the flavor of these stewed tomatoes is worth the extra effort."

John E. Sisson—Leelanau Country Inn, Maple City

5 large ripe GARDEN TOMATOES
3 Tbsp. CANOLA OIL
1 cup thinly sliced ONION
1 tsp. GARLIC PURÉE
1/2 tsp. dried BASIL
1/2 tsp. dried OREGANO

Place tomatoes in a saucepan and cover with water. Bring to a boil and cook until tomato skins begin to split. Remove tomatoes from hot water and plunge into a cold water bath. Peel tomatoes and set aside. Place one tomato in blender and purée. In a saucepan, heat oil and add sliced onions, garlic purée, basil and oregano and sauté until very tender but not browned. Add tomato purée. Quarter remaining tomatoes and place in a casserole dish. Top with sautéed onion mixture, cover and bake in a 350° oven for 15 to 20 minutes.

Serves 4.

Glorified Rice

Ellen Colburn—Brooklyn

1 pkg. (3 oz.) RASPBERRY GELATIN
2 pkg. (3 oz.) STRAWBERRY GELATIN
1 can (20 oz.) crushed PINEAPPLE, drained, juice reserved
2 cups cooked RICE
1/2 cup chopped ENGLISH WALNUTS
2 cups MINIATURE MARSHMALLOWS
1 pt. whipped, sweetened CREAM

Prepare gelatins using reserved pineapple juice and cold water. Blend in rice and walnuts and refrigerate until thickened. Combine the marshmallows and cream and fold into the gelatin mixture. Cover and refrigerate until ready to serve.

Serves 6-8.

Baby Spring Greens with Blackberry Vinaigrette

Kate & Barbara Vilter—The Riverside Inn (Chef Thomas Sawyer), Leland

mixed **BABY SPRING GREENS**
2 cups WALNUTS
4 oz. GOAT CHEESE

2 GRANNY SMITH APPLES,
halved and thinly sliced

Toss greens with ***Blackberry Vinaigrette.*** Divide between serving plates. Crumble goat cheese and walnuts over top. Arrange three apple slices on either side of plate. Serve immediately.

Serves 4.

Blackberry Vinaigrette

juice of 1/4 ORANGE
2 tsp. ORANGE ZEST
juice of 1/4 LIME
1/8 cup WATER
1/4 cup BALSAMIC VINEGAR
2 Tbsp. DICKINSON'S® BLACKBERRY JAM
1 tsp. minced GARLIC
1 tsp. cracked BLACK PEPPER
1/4 JALAPEÑO PEPPER, seeded, finely minced
SALT and PEPPER to taste
1/2 cup WALNUT OIL

Place all ingredients except oil in a blender. Blend until frothy. Add walnut oil and blend until incorporated.

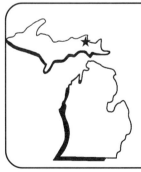

Tahquamenon Falls State Park

Tahquamenon Falls State Park, in the Upper Peninsula on the east side of Whitefish Bay was described in Longfellow's *The Song of Hiawatha.* This area is rich in natural beauty and Indian legend.

Apple Bread Stuffing

"This stuffing may be used for poultry or pork, including chops, crown roasts and rolled roasts. The addition of dried, tart cherries gives this stuffing another dimension. Also, try herbed, rye or whole wheat bread to add variety."

John E. Sisson—Leelanau Country Inn, Maple City

4 cups WATER
4 tsp. Wyler's® CHICKEN BOUILLON
1 cup diced ONIONS
1 cup diced CELERY
2 cups sliced APPLES
1 Tbsp. ground CINNAMON
1 Tbsp. POULTRY SEASONING
4 cups dried BREAD cut into 1/4-inch cubes

In a deep saucepan or soup pot, mix water and chicken bouillon; then add onions, celery, apples, cinnamon and poultry seasoning, and bring to a boil. Add bread cubes, stir thoroughly, cool and refrigerate until ready to use.

Yields 4 cups stuffing.

Note: This stuffing will keep under refrigeration for up to 2 weeks, or can be frozen and held for up to 6 months. When using frozen stuffing, allow to thaw, and check moisture content—a small addition of water may be necessary. Vary the amount of bread used to increase or decrease the moistness of the stuffing.

Zucchini Casserole

3 cups SLICED ZUCCHINI
1/2 cup crushed SALTINE
   CRACKERS
3 EGGS, beaten
1/2 tsp. SALT

1/2 cup melted BUTTER
1 cup MILK
2 cups shredded CHEDDAR
   CHEESE

Preheat oven to 300°. Combine all ingredients well in a large mixing bowl. Place mixture in a lightly greased casserole dish and bake uncovered, for 30-40 minutes.

Serves 4-6.

Dandelion Greens

"Gather greens in early spring before flower buds develop."

Dorris Stoll—North Adams

4 Tbsp. FLOUR
1 tsp. SALT
2 Tbsp. SUGAR
3 Tbsp. VINEGAR
1 1/2 cups WATER

4 slices BACON, chopped
2 EGGS, hard-boiled, chopped
4 cups washed and chopped
   DANDELION GREENS

In a bowl, combine flour, salt, sugar, vinegar and water. In a skillet, cook bacon until crisp. Remove and reserve bacon. Add the flour mixture to skillet and cook until thickened. Add chopped eggs, dandelion greens and bacon. Heat and serve.

Serves 4.

Muskegon

Once known as the Lumber Queen of the World, Muskegon is the largest city on the eastern shore of Lake Michigan. Over 3,000 acres of recreational land include the Pere Marquette Park, Muskegon State Park and the P.J. Hoffmaster State Park.

Bean Pie

"A lot of beans are raised in Michigan. Here is a tasty way to use them."

Dorris Stoll—North Adams

2 cups cooked NAVY BEANS, mashed
1/2 cup MILK
1 cup SUGAR
2 EGGS, well beaten

1/3 stick BUTTER
1/2 tsp. VANILLA
dash of NUTMEG
unbaked PIE CRUST

Preheat oven to 425°. Combine all ingredients, place in pie crust and bake for 10 minutes at 425°, then 30 minutes at 325°.

Serves 6.

Copper Pennies

This is a great vegetable dish to make ahead of time for pot luck dinners.

2 lbs. CARROTS, peeled
   and sliced 1/2" thick
1/2 cup VINEGAR
1/4 cup VEGETABLE OIL

1/3 cup SUGAR
1 can (10.75 oz.) TOMATO SOUP
1 GREEN BELL PEPPER, chopped
1 ONION, sliced into rings

In a saucepan, cover carrots with water and cook until just tender. In another saucepan, combine the vinegar, oil, sugar and soup and bring to a boil. Place carrots, bell pepper and onion rings in a large ceramic or glass bowl and cover with the vinegar mixture. Store in refrigerator for several hours before serving.

Serves 6.

Potatoes Whipped with Sour Cream & Herbs

Mary Jo Henrickson—Elmhurst Bed & Breakfast, Shelby

3 cups WATER
1 1/2 cups MILK
1 stick MARGARINE or BUTTER
3/4 tsp. SALT
1 cup SOUR CREAM
1 cup chopped fresh HERBS (dill, chives, parsley, finely
   chopped green onions or any combination)
4 cups uncooked INSTANT MASHED POTATOES
PARMESAN CHEESE

In a medium saucepan, bring to a boil the water, milk, margarine (or butter) and salt. Remove pan from heat; add sour cream, herbs and instant potatoes; blend thoroughly. Place mixture in a broilerproof oiled serving dish and sprinkle top with Parmesan cheese. Brown under broiler. Garnish with additional herbs.

Serves 8-12.

Easy Sour Cream Blueberry Muffins

"Our guests love these muffins."

Robert & Doris Knapp—All Decked Out Country Cottage,
Maple City

1 1/4 cups SUGAR
2 cups FLOUR
1 tsp. BAKING POWDER
1/2 tsp. BAKING SODA
1/4 tsp. SALT

1/2 cup MARGARINE
2 EGGS
1 cup SOUR CREAM
1 tsp. VANILLA
2 cups BLUEBERRIES

Preheat oven to 400° Mix all ingredients in order listed except blueberries. Fold blueberries into batter. Lightly oil 24 muffin cups and fill cups 3/4 full. Sprinkle sugar on tops. Bake for 25-30 minutes.

Lemon-Poppy Seed Bread

Laurie Vandermeulen—Kentwood

1 box LEMON CAKE MIX
1 pkg. (3 oz.) COCONUT PUDDING
1/2 cup MARGARINE, melted (or use OIL)
4 EGGS
1/8 cup POPPY SEEDS
1 cup HOT WATER

Preheat oven to 350°. Beat together for 2 minutes. Put into 2 greased and floured loaf pans. Bake for 40-45 minutes.

Multigrain Bread

This bread has a nice nutty flavor and is especially delicious toasted.

Donna Hodge—Bed & Breakfast at The Pines, Frankenmuth

1 1/2 cups boiling WATER
1 cup MULTIGRAIN CEREAL
2 pkgs. DRY YEAST
1/2 cup WARM WATER
6 Tbsp. SALAD OIL
2 EGGS, unbeaten
1 cup WHOLE WHEAT FLOUR
1/2 cup HONEY
SALT to taste
4 to 4 1/2 cups ALL-PURPOSE FLOUR

Pour boiling water over multigrain cereal in a large mixing bowl; set aside to cool. Dissolve yeast in 1/2 cup warm water. When cereal is lukewarm, add yeast and all remaining ingredients except all-purpose flour. Blend thoroughly and then add flour. Knead on floured board until smooth. Place in a greased bowl and let double. Punch down and divide in half. Shape into loaves and place in greased bread pans. Grease top of bread lightly, cover and let rise until almost double. Preheat oven to 375°. Bake for 40 to 45 minutes. Remove from pans and cool.

Honey-Wheat Buns

"At our working farm bed-and-breakfast we serve fresh Michigan-grown foods. As we grow wheat, I do most all of the baking from scratch. Our honey comes from our daughter-in-law who is a beekeeper."

Sue Chaffin—Chaffin Balmoral Farm Bed & Breakfast, Ithaca

2 cups ALL-PURPOSE FLOUR
1 cup WHOLE WHEAT FLOUR
2 pkgs. DRY YEAST
1 Tbsp. SALT
1 cup MILK
1 cup WATER
1/2 cup HONEY
3 Tbsp. OIL
1 EGG, beaten
1 1/2 cups WHOLE WHEAT FLOUR
1 1/2 to 2 cups ALL-PURPOSE FLOUR

Combine both flours, yeast and salt in a large bowl; mix well. In a saucepan, heat milk, water, honey and oil until very warm. Add to flour mixture; then add egg. Blend all with electric mixer, then beat for 3 minutes. Stir in whole wheat flour and enough all-purpose flour to make a firm dough. Knead for 5-8 minutes. Place in a greased bowl and turn. Cover and let rise until double. Punch down and let rest. Shape into 24 buns and place on greased, covered pans. Let rise again. Preheat oven to 375° and bake for 20 minutes.

Makes 24 buns.

Did you know?

"The Cross in the Woods," the world's largest crucifix, may be seen at Indian River (just 1 mile west of I-75 and about 25 miles south of the Mackinac Bridge). This 55-foot-high cross is made of one California redwood tree and weighs 21 tons. The museum at this site features over 500 nun and priest dolls dressed in the costumes of a variety of religious orders.

Bavarian Town Eight-Week Muffins

"We make the batter for these muffins and store it in the refrigerator, using portions as needed for as long as eight weeks!"

Louie & Kathy Weiss—Bavarian Town Bed & Breakfast, Frankenmuth

1 box (15 oz.) RAISIN BRAN
3 cups SUGAR
5 cups FLOUR
4 tsp. BAKING SODA
2 tsp. SALT
1 tsp. CINNAMON

4 EGGS
1 qt. BUTTERMILK
1 cup SAFFLOWER OIL
1 tsp. VANILLA
MICHIGAN HICKORY NUTS
MICHIGAN DRIED CHERRIES

In large bowl, mix first 6 ingredients with spoon. In another large bowl beat the eggs. Add buttermilk, oil and vanilla to eggs and beat well. Add egg mixture to dry mixture and mix well with spoon. Store in a covered container in refrigerator for at least 8 hours before using. Preheat oven to 350°. Prior to filling muffin cups (2/3 full) mix in nuts and dried cherries. Bake for 20 minutes for mini-muffin tins (add 5 minutes for regular-size tins, or 10 minutes for large).

Blueberry Muffins

Donna Hodge—Bed & Breakfast at The Pines, Frankenmuth

1 1/2 cups ALL-PURPOSE FLOUR
1/2 cup SUGAR
2 tsp. BAKING POWDER
1/2 tsp. SALT

1 EGG
1/2 cup MILK
1/4 cup OIL
1 cup BLUEBERRIES

Preheat oven to 400°. In a large mixing bowl, sift together the flour, sugar, baking powder and salt. In another bowl, blend together the egg, milk and oil. Mix egg mixture with dry mixture just until ingredients are blended. Fold in blueberries. Fill greased muffin cups 2/3 full. Bake for 20-25 minutes or until golden brown.

Makes 12 muffins.

Almond-Peach Yogurt Bread

Judy-Kern Bertram—The Lamplighter Bed & Breakfast,
Ludington

3 cups ALL-PURPOSE FLOUR
1 tsp. SALT
1 tsp. BAKING SODA
1/2 tsp. BAKING POWDER
3 EGGS
1 cup VEGETABLE OIL
1 1/2 cups SUGAR
2 cups PEACH YOGURT
1 Tbsp. ALMOND EXTRACT
1/2 cup ALMONDS, sliced, optional

Preheat oven to 325°. Measure, sift and mix the dry ingredients into a large bowl. Lightly beat the eggs in another large bowl. Add the oil and sugar to the eggs and blend well. Mix in the yogurt and almond extract. Add this mixture to the dry ingredients, add nuts and mix until just combined. Pour into 2 well-greased loaf pans. Bake for approximately 1 hour.

Banana Bread

Marie Myers—Jackson

2 1/4 cups FLOUR
1 Tbsp. BAKING POWDER
1/2 tsp. BAKING SODA
1 tsp. SALT
1/2 cup SHORTENING

1 cup SUGAR
2 EGGS, beaten
3 med. BANANAS, mashed
1/4 cup chopped NUTS

Preheat oven to 375°. Sift flour, baking powder, baking soda and salt together. Cream together the shortening and sugar. Add eggs and blend. Add bananas and flour mixture alternately, mixing until well blended. Fold in nuts. Pour into a large, greased loaf pan and bake for 1 hour or until tests done. Cool and slice.

Apple-Cranberry Muffins

Ric and Mary Ellen Postlewaite—Garden Grove Bed & Breakfast,
Union Pier

2 cups FLOUR
1/2 cup SUGAR
1 Tbsp. BAKING POWDER
1/2 tsp. SALT
1/2 tsp. CINNAMON
1 EGG, lightly beaten
4 Tbsp. BUTTER, melted
1 cup MILK
1 sm. COOKING APPLE, peeled and diced
1/2 cup chopped CRANBERRIES
1/2 cup chopped WALNUTS
CINNAMON SUGAR

Preheat oven to 375°. Mix dry ingredients. Add egg, butter and milk. Stir just until dry ingredients are moistened. Fold in apple, cranberries and walnuts. Sprinkle tops with *Cinnamon Sugar.* Spoon into greased muffin cups and bake for 25 to 30 minutes, or until edges of muffins start to brown.

Makes 12 muffins.

Cinnamon Sugar

1/2 cup SUGAR   1 tsp. CINNAMON

Combine sugar and cinnamon in a small bowl.

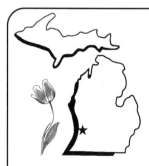

Holland

Founded by Dutch immigrants in 1847, this city's Tulip Time Festival in May is world renowned. Holland maintains its Dutch essence to this day. Explore the 30-acre Windmill Island Park here and enjoy its unusual miniature Dutch village, extensive tulip gardens, drawbridge and an operating 1780s windmill brought from the Netherlands.

Blueberry Tea Bread

"I serve blueberries often and purchase them in 10-pound boxes in season. I also make this bread from the frozen blueberries that I have premeasured before freezing. Friends and guests are always asking for this recipe. You can bake it one day and serve it the next day. It freezes very well."

Shirley Piepenburg—Deer Lake Bed & Breakfast, Boyne City

3 cups ALL-PURPOSE FLOUR
1 cup SUGAR
2 tsp. BAKING POWDER
1/2 tsp. SALT
1/2 cup (1 stick) LIGHT MARGARINE
1 cup SKIM or LOW FAT MILK
1 tsp. VANILLA EXTRACT
1 tsp. ALMOND EXTRACT
1 lg. EGG, beaten
1 1/2 cups BLUEBERRIES

Preheat oven to 350°. In large bowl, combine flour, sugar, baking powder and salt. With pastry blender, cut margarine into flour mixture until mixture resembles fine crumbs. Stir in milk, extracts and egg until flour is just moistened. Gently stir in blueberries. Spoon batter into a greased 9 x 5 loaf pan. Sprinkle ***Crumb Topping*** over batter. Bake loaf 1 hour 25 minutes or until toothpick inserted in center comes out clean. Cool loaf in pan on wire rack 10 minutes; remove from pan and finish cooling on rack.

Crumb Topping

1 Tbsp. SLIVERED ALMONDS   **2 Tbsp. SUGAR**
1/2 tsp. ground CINNAMON   **1 Tbsp. MARGARINE**
2 Tbsp. FLOUR

In small bowl, combine all ingredients and blend with a fork until mixture resembles coarse crumbs.

Apple-Pecan Muffins

"I prefer to use local ingredients, so our guests can get the freshest tastes and flavors. This recipe was designed with our abundant apple harvests in mind."

Mrs. Chris Mason—The Parish House Inn, Ypsilanti

3 cups ALL-PURPOSE FLOUR
1/2 tsp. BAKING POWDER
1 tsp. BAKING SODA
1/2 tsp. SALT
1/2 tsp. ground CLOVES
4 EGGS, beaten
2 cups SUGAR
1 cup OIL
1 Tbsp. VANILLA
3 cups peeled and finely chopped APPLES
2/3 cup RAISINS
1/2 cup chopped PECANS

Preheat oven to 400°. In a large mixing bowl, stir together flour, baking powder, baking soda, salt and cloves. In medium bowl, mix together eggs, sugar, oil and vanilla. Add egg mixture to dry ingredients. Fold in apples, raisins and nuts, stirring until just moist. Line cups of two 12-cup muffin tins with paper baking cups. Spoon batter into cups until 2/3 full. Bake for 15 to 20 minutes or until test done. Serve warm or cool.

Makes 24 muffins.

Note: These keep in the refrigerator for 2 to 3 days. You may substitute cinnamon or nutmeg for cloves.

Saginaw

Fur trading and then lumbering were the first commercial operations of this city. Today, Saginaw is a manufacturing city with many industrial plants. Sugar beets and beans are also important commodities here.

DESSERTS & BEVERAGES

Pineapple Cookies

*"This recipe was given to me by my mother,
Mrs. Foster Murray."*

Sharon Dexter—Napoleon

1 cup BUTTER	4 cups FLOUR
1 cup packed BROWN SUGAR	1 tsp. BAKING SODA
1 cup WHITE SUGAR	1 can (20 oz.) CRUSHED
2 EGGS	PINEAPPLE, drained
2 tsp. VANILLA	1 cup chopped NUTS

Preheat oven to 350°. Cream butter, sugars, eggs and vanilla together. Sift flour and baking soda together and add to butter mixture alternately with pineapple. Add nuts. Drop by teaspoonful onto a greased cookie sheet. Bake for 12 minutes.

Makes 5 dozen cookies.

Evelyn's Sugar Cookies

Evelyn Hollingshead—Jackson

2 cups WHITE or packed BROWN SUGAR
1 cup SHORTENING
1 tsp. BAKING SODA
1 cup SOUR CREAM or MILK
1/2 tsp. SALT
2 EGGS, beaten
1 tsp. BAKING POWDER
1 tsp. VANILLA
4-6 cups FLOUR

Preheat oven to 400°. Cream together the sugar and shortening. Dissolve baking soda in sour cream or milk. Combine mixtures, then add salt, eggs, baking powder and vanilla. Add enough flour to allow dough to be rolled out. Roll to 1/2-inch thickness. Cut out cookies with cookie cutters. Bake on greased cookie sheets for 10-12 minutes or until light brown.

Makes 6 dozen cookies.

Chocolate Oatmeal Quickies

Sonia Birch—Jackson

5 Tbsp. COCOA
2 cups SUGAR
1/2 cup BUTTER
1/2 cup MILK
3 1/2 cups QUICK-COOKING OATS
1 tsp. VANILLA
1 cup COCONUT FLAKES

Mix cocoa, sugar, butter and milk together in a 3-quart saucepan. Bring to a boil, stirring constantly to prevent scorching. Boil for 1 minute. Stir in oats, vanilla and coconut. Drop by teaspoonfuls onto waxed paper and chill.

Makes 4 dozen.

Ranger Cookies

Clara Bostwick—Jackson

2 cups SHORTENING
2 cups WHITE SUGAR
2 cups packed BROWN SUGAR
4 EGGS
2 tsp. VANILLA
4 cups FLOUR
1 tsp. BAKING SODA
1 tsp. BAKING POWDER
2 cups RICE KRISPIES®
2 cups COCONUT FLAKES

Preheat oven to 350°. Cream shortening and sugars together. Add eggs, vanilla, flour, baking soda and baking powder. Blend. Fold in Rice Krispies and coconut flakes. Mold into 1 1/2-inch balls and place on a greased cookie sheet. Press each down lightly. Bake about 12 minutes.

Makes about 5 dozen cookies.

Sweet Potato Pie

1 (9-inch) unbaked PIE CRUST
2 cups mashed cooked SWEET POTATOES
1 cup packed BROWN SUGAR
1/2 stick BUTTER, melted
2 EGGS, beaten
1 cup HALF & HALF
1 tsp. CINNAMON
1/2 tsp. ALLSPICE
1 Tbsp. LEMON JUICE

Preheat oven to 400°. Bake crust for 15 minutes. In a large bowl, blend sweet potatoes with brown sugar; add melted butter, mixing well. Mix in eggs and half & half. Add remaining ingredients, blending well. Reduce oven temperature to 350°. Pour mixture into pie crust. Bake 30 to 40 minutes or until pie is set.

Orange Cookies

Virginia Dexter—Spring Arbor

2/3 cup SHORTENING
3/4 cup SUGAR
1 EGG
1/2 cup ORANGE JUICE
2 Tbsp. grated ORANGE RIND

2 cups FLOUR
1/2 tsp. SODA
1/2 tsp. BAKING POWDER
1/2 tsp. SALT

Preheat oven to 400°. Cream shortening and sugar together. Add egg, juice and rind. Combine remaining ingredients and add to dough. Drop by teaspoonfuls onto an ungreased cookie sheet. Bake for 8-10 minutes. Remove from oven and while still warm, ice with *Orange Frosting*.

Makes 2 dozen cookies.

Orange Frosting

1 cup POWDERED SUGAR, sifted
1/8 tsp. SALT

2 Tbsp. BUTTER
1 1/2 Tbsp. ORANGE JUICE

Combine all ingredients until smooth.

Pumpkin Cookies

Miriam Billings—Fountain

1 cup packed BROWN SUGAR
1/4 cup WHITE SUGAR
1/2 cup SHORTENING
2 EGGS, lighty beaten
2 cups cooked PUMPKIN, mashed
1/2 tsp. SALT
1/2 tsp. CINNAMON
1/2 tsp. NUTMEG

1/2 tsp. ground GINGER
2 1/2 cups FLOUR
4 tsp. BAKING POWDER
1 cup RAISINS
1 cup chopped NUTS
1 tsp. VANILLA
1 tsp. LEMON EXTRACT

Preheat oven to 375°. Cream brown and white sugar with shortening. Add eggs and pumpkin to sugar mixture. Add salt and spices, blend well. Sift and resift flour and baking powder together. Add raisins and nuts to flour and beat into sugar mixture. Add vanilla and lemon extract, and blend. Drop by teaspoonfuls onto greased cookie sheet and bake for 20 minutes.

Makes 4 dozen cookies.

Pecan Squares

Verna McCollum—Jackson

1/3 cup SHORTENING
1/3 cup BUTTER, softened
1 tsp. BAKING POWDER
1 EGG, well beaten

3/4 cup SUGAR
1 3/4 cup FLOUR
1/2 tsp. SALT
1 tsp. VANILLA

Preheat oven to 375°. Mix on low speed with electric mixer until beaters gather dough together (2 minutes). Spread mixture on a greased cookie sheet. Bake 10 minutes. Remove from oven and spread with *Pecan Topping.* Bake for 20 to 25 minutes more. Cut into squares.

Pecan Topping

2 EGGS, lightly beaten
1 1/2 cups chopped PECANS

2 cups (packed) BROWN SUGAR
4 Tbsp. FLOUR

Combine all ingredients together until smooth.

Cherry Pudding Cake

"I also serve this cake at breakfast and the guests love it!"

Virginia Boegner—The Ludington House 1878 Victorian Bed & Breakfast, Ludington

2 qts. fresh RED SOUR CHERRIES, pitted
2 1/2 cups SUGAR, divided
1/8 tsp. ALMOND EXTRACT
2 cups FLOUR
4 tsp. BAKING POWDER
1 cup MILK
2 Tbsp. VEGETABLE OIL
WHIPPED CREAM or ICE CREAM

Preheat oven to 375°. In a large bowl, combine cherries with 1 1/2 cups of sugar and the almond extract. Set aside. In another bowl, combine flour, 1 cup sugar, baking powder, milk and oil; mix well and pour into a greased 9 x 13 baking pan. Spoon cherry mixture over batter. Bake for 40-45 minutes or until tests done. Serve warm with whipped cream or ice cream.

Serves 12-14.

Cream Rhubarb Pie

*"My mother, Mae Howard, gave me this recipe.
I make it quite often."*

Verna McCollum—Jackson

2 cups cut-up RHUBARB
3/4 cup SUGAR
1 cup MILK
2 EGG YOLKS

1/4 cup SUGAR
2 Tbsp. CORNSTARCH
1/4 tsp. SALT
baked PIE SHELL

Preheat oven to 350°. In a saucepan, combine rhubarb and sugar; stew until rhubarb is soft. Combine milk, egg yolks, sugar, cornstarch and salt. Add to rhubarb mixture and cook, stirring constantly, until mixture thickens to a custard consistency. Cool, pour into pie shell and bake for 15 minutes. Increase oven temperature to 375°. Swirl **Meringue** over top of pie and bake 8 to 10 minutes longer or until lightly browned.

Meringue

3 EGG WHITES
1/4 tsp. CREAM OF TARTAR
6 Tbsp. SUGAR

Beat egg whites with cream of tartar until frothy. Beat sugar in gradually, a little at a time. Continue beating until mixture is stiff and glossy and sugar is dissolved.

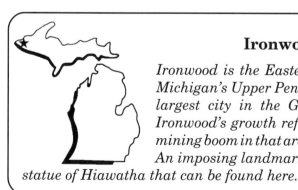

Ironwood

Ironwood is the Easternmost city of Michigan's Upper Peninsula and the largest city in the Gogebic Range. Ironwood's growth reflected the iron mining boom in that area in the 1880s. An imposing landmark is the 52-foot statue of Hiawatha that can be found here.

Crazy, Lazy Chocolate Cake

"I like to keep fruits and muffins and some sort of cake on my sideboard for my guests to help themselves anytime. This cake is especially liked and is a no-cholesterol dessert! This is an amazingly firm, rich, eggless chocolate cake. "

Shirley Boutwell—Cider House Bed and Breakfast, Traverse City

3 cups ALL-PURPOSE FLOUR, unsifted
1 1/2 cups granulated SUGAR
1 tsp. SALT
2 tsp. SODA
1/3 cup COCOA
2/3 cup CORN OIL
1 tsp. VANILLA
2 Tbsp. APPLE CIDER VINEGAR
2 cups cold WATER

Preheat oven to 350°. Add all of the ingredients to a 3-quart electric mixer bowl. Mix with electric mixer or whisk for about 3 minutes or until well blended. Pour into greased 9 x 13 baking dish and bake for 40 minutes or until tests done.

Soft Sour Cream Cookies

Donna Hodge—Bed & Breakfast at The Pines, Frankenmuth

1 2/3 cups WHITE SUGAR
1 cup SHORTENING
2 EGGS, unbeaten
1 tsp. VANILLA
4 1/2 cups ALL-PURPOSE
   FLOUR, sifted
1/2 tsp. BAKING POWDER
1 tsp. SODA
1 tsp. SALT
1 tsp. NUTMEG
1 cup SOUR CREAM
1 Tbsp. LEMON JUICE

Cream sugar and shortening together until fluffy. Add eggs and vanilla. Continue mixing. Sift together the dry ingredients and add alternately with sour cream and lemon juice to sugar mixture. Chill dough. Roll out on a floured surface, cut with floured cookie cutter. Preheat oven to 375°. Place cookies on a greased cookie sheet and sprinkle with sugar. Bake for 10-12 minutes.

Makes about 3 1/2 dozen 3-inch cookies.

Rhubarb Coffee Cake

"Nestled in the heart of Leelenau wine country, Omena Shores is a renovated barn, built in 1852 as part of the Omena Presbyterian Church parsonage."

Omena Shores Bed & Breakfast—Omena

1/2 cup BUTTER
1 1/4 cups SUGAR
1 EGG
2 cups FLOUR
1 tsp. BAKING SODA

1/2 tsp. SALT
1 cup BUTTERMILK
1 tsp. VANILLA
2 cups chopped RHUBARB

Preheat oven to 350°. Grease a 9 x 13 square cake pan or two 9-inch round cake pans. Cream butter and sugar until light; beat in egg. Add dry ingredients to creamed mixture alternately with buttermilk. Fold in vanilla and rhubarb. Pour into baking pan. Sprinkle ***Cinnamon Topping*** over batter. Bake for 40 minutes.

Cinnamon Topping

1 tsp. CINNAMON
1/2 cup SUGAR

2 Tbsp. BUTTER, softened
1/2 cup chopped NUTS

Combine cinnamon, sugar and butter. Fold in nuts.

Fried Apples

"I am especially fond of Paula Red apples. They had their beginning in Sparta, Michigan, where we once lived."

Pauline E. Spray—Lapeer

Allow 2 APPLES per person

Peel and slice 2 apples for each serving desired. Place slices in a frying pan which has been sprayed with vegetable oil. Sprinkle with **SUGAR** and **CINNAMON** to taste. Stirring often, cook apples until tender. Serve, topped with **COOL WHIP** or **ICE CREAM**.

Pumpkin Roll

Paula Bedell—Munith

3 EGGS, well beaten
1 cup SUGAR
2/3 cup canned PUMPKIN
1 tsp. LEMON JUICE
3/4 cup ALL-PURPOSE FLOUR
1 tsp. BAKING POWDER

2 tsp. CINNAMON
1 tsp. GINGER
1/2 tsp. NUTMEG
1/2 tsp. SALT
1/2 cup chopped WALNUTS

Preheat oven to 375°. Combine eggs and sugar and then gradually stir in the pumpkin. Add lemon juice. Combine flour with balance of ingredients (except walnuts). Fold flour mixture into pumpkin mixture and spread on a greased cookie sheet. Sprinkle top with walnuts. Bake for 15 minutes. Let cool. Sprinkle cheesecloth with powdered sugar. Place baked pumpkin dough upside down on cheesecloth. Spread *Cream Cheese Filling* on top. Use cheesecloth to help roll dough up while still warm. Cover with aluminum foil and chill overnight. To serve, unroll, remove cheesecloth and reroll. Cut into 3/4-inch slices.

Cream Cheese Filling

1 cup POWDERED SUGAR
1 8 oz. pkg. CREAM CHEESE

4 Tbsp. BUTTER
1/2 Tbsp. VANILLA

Combine all ingredients and beat until smooth.

Jackson

Jackson is a manufacturing city in the heart of the rich farmlands of southern Michigan. Intersected by the Grand River, the original settlement, named for General Andrew Jackson, became a city in 1857. In 1854, the Republican Party was formally named at a convention held here.

Mama Esther's Baked Custard

"A family favorite. My grandmother was Swedish and she loved to cook. I also serve this recipe for breakfast."

Bonnie McVoy-Verwys—Bonnie's Parsonage 1908 Bed & Breakfast, Holland

3 EGGS, beaten
1/2 cup SUGAR
3 cups MILK (2% can be used)
GROUND NUTMEG

Preheat oven to 300°. Combine eggs, sugar and milk. Pour into 6 ramekins and sprinkle nutmeg over tops. Set dishes in pan of water to ensure custard bakes evenly. Bake for 1 1/4 hours or until sharp knife inserted in custard comes out clean. Cool and refrigerate. Custard is good plain and/or served topped with fresh strawberries, along with traditional Dutch pigs-in-the-blanket, muffins, juice and a gourmet blend coffee.

Serves 6.

Butterscotch Cake

Joyce Yelton—Carriage House Park & Harbor, South Haven

1 1/4 cups WATER
2/3 cup BUTTERSCOTCH PIECES
1 pkg. YELLOW or CARAMEL CAKE MIX
3 EGGS
1/3 cup COOKING OIL
1/8 tsp. ground CINNAMON

Preheat oven to 350°. Heat water and butterscotch pieces until pieces are melted. Cool for 10 minutes. Grease and flour bundt pan. In a large bowl, combine cake mix, eggs, oil, cinnamon and butterscotch mixture; beat with electric mixer as directed for cake mix. Pour into bundt pan. Bake for 25-30 minutes or until tests done. Cool on rack for 10 minutes, remove from pan, cool completely on wire rack before frosting with your favorite butterscotch frosting.

Lemon-Lime Tofu Cheesecake

"In order to regain good health, many of my favorite rich desserts had to go. My most favorite was lemon-lime cheesecake. This revised recipe has satisfied my tastebuds and become a favorite of those with whom I have shared it."

Sandra Stewart—Saginaw

Crust:
- 1 cup GRAPE NUTS®, ground
- 1/8 cup APPLE JUICE CONCENTRATE
- 1 Tbsp. SPECTRUM SPREAD (butter substitute)
- 1 Tbsp. FRUCTOSE

Preheat oven to 325°. Grind Grape Nuts in blender. Pour into a small bowl. Add remaining ingredients and mix thoroughly. Press into a sprayed 9-inch pie plate and bake for 10 minutes. Set aside to cool.

Filling:
- 2 boxes extra-firm TOFU
- 2/3 cup FRUCTOSE
- 2 Tbsp. fresh LEMON JUICE
- 2 Tbsp. fresh LIME JUICE
- 2 Tbsp. TOFUTTI® SOUR SUPREME (sour cream substitute)

Place above ingredients in blender. Blend until smooth. Pour into cooled crust and freeze. Remove from freezer 1/2 hour before serving.

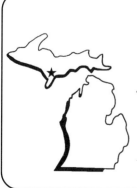

Escanaba

The logging boom of the 1880s and the deepwater harbor at the mouth of the Escanaba River contributed much to the growth of this Upper Peninsula city. Second-growth trees, iron mining and an ever growing tourist trade continue to make this a prosperous place to live. Many visitors come just to see the nearby 1867 Sandpoint Lighthouse.

Mrs. Palm's Pear Pie

"My mother, Mrs. Willie Lee Palm, created this original recipe about 50 years ago. My parents have a large backyard in Detroit where two beautiful pear trees produce a lovely bountiful harvest every year. Our entire family has helped harvest these trees down through these years, and my mother still bakes this delicious pear pie that the family and many friends crave."

Wanda J. Burnside—Detroit

2 cups ALL-PURPOSE FLOUR
3/4 cup SHORTENING
5 Tbsp. COLD WATER

Preheat oven to 350° Add flour to a medium-size mixing bowl. Cut shortening into flour to a coarse consistency. Gradually sprinkle in water, a tablespoon at a time. Continue to blend and add water until an elastic dough is formed. Divide dough in half, making two balls. Flour waxed paper or use floured cheesecloth and roll out dough for two 9-inch crusts. Set aside.

Fresh Pear Pie Filling

4 cups fresh firm PEARS (about 7 medium)
1 tsp. CINNAMON
2 tsp. NUTMEG
1 tsp. VANILLA FLAVORING
1 1/2 cups SUGAR
3 Tbsp. ALL-PURPOSE FLOUR

Peel and slice pears, rinse in cold water and drain well. Place pears in a bowl and sprinkle cinnamon and nutmeg evenly over top. Dot with vanilla. Spread sugar evenly over all, sprinkle with flour and gently combine.

1 stick BUTTER or MARGARINE, sliced
3 tsp. GRANULATED SUGAR

Place ***Fresh Pear Pie Filling*** in pie shell. Place sliced butter or margarine on top of filling mixture (reserving two slices). Cover filling with top crust and seal edges. Cut slits in top crust. Bake for 20 minutes at 350°, then increase oven temperature to 400° and continue baking for 15-20 minutes to brown. Let cool for 5 minutes. Melt remaining butter, brush over top of crust and sprinkle with sugar.

Delicious Caramels

Harbor House Inn—Grand Haven

1 cup granulated SUGAR
1 cup DARK KARO® SYRUP
1 cup BUTTER
1 can (14 oz.) SWEETENED CONDENSED MILK
1 tsp. VANILLA

In a medium saucepan, mix sugar, syrup and butter over medium heat. (Be sure heat is not too high or caramels will be hard.) Continue stirring until the mixture comes to a "ploppy" boil. Time for 7 minutes, no stirring. Add condensed milk. Mix well, and continue stirring over medium heat. When the mixture comes to a "ploppy" boil again, time for 13 minutes, stirring constantly. Remove from heat, add vanilla, mix well and pour into well-buttered 8 x 8 glass pan. Cool overnight at room temperature. Cut into bite-size squares and wrap. Makes approximately 70 caramels.

Holiday Sugar Cookies

Diane M. Hubbell—Hillsdale

2 sticks MARGARINE
1 cup SUGAR
1 1/2 tsp. VANILLA
1 EGG

1 Tbsp. WATER
3 cups FLOUR
1 1/2 tsp. BAKING POWDER
1/4 tsp. SALT

Preheat oven to 375°. Thoroughly cream margarine, sugar and vanilla. Add egg and water. Beat until light and fluffy. Combine flour, baking powder and salt. Blend into creamed mixture. Divide dough in half and chill 1 hour. On a lightly floured surface roll dough to 1/8-inch thickness. Cut into desired shapes. If desired, brush lightly with milk and sprinkle with colored sugar, or, after baking, frost with your favorite cookie frosting. Bake on greased cookie sheet 6-8 minutes. Do not overbake. Cool slightly. Transfer from pan to paper towel.

Makes 5 dozen cookies.

Pineapple Cheesecake

"My grandmother always made this dessert when she knew I was coming to visit. I never thought of asking her for the recipe, then after she passed away, I wanted badly to taste her wonderful cake but no one had the recipe. I called my cousin and between the two of us, we were able to remember the ingredients. It tastes just about the way I remembered it."

Marilyn Secord—Yesterday Once More Country Heritage Bed & Breakfast, Romeo

1 cup boiling WATER
1 box (6 oz.) LEMON GELATIN
1 pkg. (8-oz.) CREAM CHEESE
1 cup SUGAR
1 can (20 oz.) crushed PINEAPPLE, drained
1 can (12 oz.) EVAPORATED MILK

Mix boiling water and gelatin in a bowl. Mix cream cheese and sugar in a second bowl. Add pineapple to cream cheese mixture. Whip for 3 minutes like whipping cream, add evaporated milk, then add gelatin mixture. Pour into prepared chilled *Graham Cracker Crust.* Sprinkle reserved 1/4 cup of graham cracker mixture over top.

Graham Cracker Crust

2 cups crushed GRAHAM
    CRACKERS
2 Tbsp. SUGAR

1/2 cup BUTTER, melted
1/2 tsp. CINNAMON

Combine ingredients and, reserving 1/4 cup, place the balance in a 9 x 13 baking pan. Refrigerate overnight.

Did you know?

Springs bubbling in the riverbed near Kalamazoo are said to be the origin of this city's name. This American Indian word, meaning "place where the water boils" became the catchy name of this southwestern city in Michigan.

Chocolate Cheesecake

"This cheesecake tastes even better when made a couple of days ahead and refrigerated, allowing the flavors to blend."

Jane E. Lovett—Peaches Bed & Breakfast, Ltd., Grand Rapids

2 1/2 cups CHOCOLATE COOKIE CRUMBS
5 Tbsp. MARGARINE, melted
4 pkgs. (8 oz. ea.) CREAM CHEESE
3/4 cup SUGAR
1 tsp. VANILLA
3 EGGS
12 oz. CHOCOLATE CHIPS, melted
1 cup SOUR CREAM
2 Tbsp. GOLD RUM
1/2 tsp. CINNAMON

Preheat oven to 325°. Grease a 9-inch springform pan. Combine crumbs and margarine, press into bottom of pan and up the sides. Beat cream cheese, sugar and vanilla until fluffy. Blend in eggs one at a time. Add melted chocolate and combine well. Add sour cream, rum and cinnamon and beat well. Pour into crust. Bake for 1 hour. Cool to room temperature and then refrigerate until cold.

Grandma Ivy's Pudding Cake

Susan B. Wojcik—Oak Cove Resort, Lawrence

1 cup FLOUR
1 cup SUGAR
1 tsp. CINNAMON
1 tsp. SODA
1 EGG

1/2 STICK BUTTER
1 can (28 oz.) FRUIT COCKTAIL, undrained
1/2 cup packed BROWN SUGAR
1/2 cup chopped WALNUTS

Preheat oven to 300°. Mix first seven ingredients together and pour into a 9 x 12 greased cake pan. Combine brown sugar and nuts in a small bowl. Sprinkle brown sugar mixture on top of cake batter. Bake for 45 minutes or until cake tests done.

Jamprints

"A favorite recipe to use up jams and jellies."

Erma Rummel—Rummel's Tree Haven Bed & Breakfast,
Sebewaing

1 1/4 cup BUTTER or MARGARINE
1 cup SUGAR
2 EGGS
2 Tbsp. VANILLA
3 cups sifted FLOUR
1/2 tsp. SALT
JAMS or JELLIES—any flavor
WALNUTS or PECANS, finely chopped

Preheat oven to 375°. Cream butter until soft; gradually add sugar, creaming well. Blend in unbeaten eggs and vanilla and beat well. Sift flour with salt, then gradually add to the creamed mixture, mixing thoroughly. Drop by rounded teaspoonful onto an ungreased cookie sheet. Make indentation in center of each, using thimble or back of teaspoon. Place jam or jelly in center of each cookie and sprinkle lightly with nuts. Bake 10-12 minutes.

Makes about 7 dozen.

Mackinac Bridge

The Mackinac Bridge connects the Lower Peninsula at Mackinaw City to the Upper Peninsula at St. Ignace. This 5-mile-long bridge is one of the longest suspension spans in the world. Every Labor Day morning some 50,000 people participate in the Mackinac Bridge Walk from St. Ignace to Mackinaw City.

Banket

"This recipe is an old family favorite, having its roots in our Dutch heritage. It was passed down to me by my mother. Bankets appear in different forms here and in the Netherlands, where a 'kerst krans' or 'Christmas crown' is made in a circle and topped with a glaze and candied fruit. Some make the filling only and wrap it in puff pastry squares to be baked and used for a scrumptious lunch cake for the kids."

Marietta Jean VanBrugge—Portage

Crust:
 1 lb. MARGARINE or BUTTER
 4 cups + 2 Tbsp. FLOUR
 1 cup COLD WATER

Mix together all ingredients. Form into a square. Wrap in waxed paper and chill overnight.

Filling:
 1 lb. ALMOND PASTE, grated
 2 EGGS
 2 cups SUGAR
 1 tsp. VANILLA

Mix together all filling ingredients. Form into a square. Wrap in waxed paper and chill overnight. When ready to bake, preheat oven to 425°. Cut crust dough into 10 pieces and filling into 20 pieces. Roll out crust dough pieces on a floured board to rectangular shapes that are 1 foot long and 5 inches wide. Roll each piece of filling between hands to make a long, thin roll about 5 1/2 inches long. Lay each piece end to end on dough, overlapping ends slightly. Flip ends of crust dough over filling and then sides. Place "sticks" on aluminum foil-covered cookie sheets, about 1 inch apart. Brush tops with **1 beaten EGG,** and pierce with a fork to let steam escape. Bake for 20 minutes.

Wacky Cocoa Cake

"Very good with peanut butter frosting."

Evelyn Hollingshead—Jackson

3 cups FLOUR
2 cups SUGAR
1/2 cup COCOA
2 tsp. BAKING SODA
1 tsp. SALT

2 cups WATER
3/4 cup VEGETABLE OIL
2 Tbsp. VINEGAR
2 tsp. VANILLA

Preheat oven to 350°. Combine flour, sugar, cocoa, soda and salt in a large mixing bowl. Add water, oil, vinegar and vanilla. Beat 3 minutes with electric mixer at medium speed until thoroughly blended. Pour batter into a 13 x 9 greased and floured baking pan. Bake 35-40 minutes or until cake tester comes out clean.

A Happy Home Recipe

"My mom received a linen dish towel that had this recipe on it for Christmas one year. She loved it! And she was all of these things."

Ellen Colburn—Brooklyn

4 cups of LOVE
2 cups of LOYALTY
4 qts. of FAITH
2 spoonsful of TENDERNESS
3 cups of FORGIVENESS

3 cups of UNDERSTANDING
1 cup of FRIENDSHIP
5 spoonsful of HOPE
1 barrel of LAUGHTER
a bushel of SUNSHINE

Take love and loyalty, mix it thoroughly with faith. Blend it with tenderness, forgiveness and understanding. Add friendship and hope. Sprinkle abundantly with laughter. Bake with sunshine and serve daily in generous helpings.

Recipe Contributors

Our sincere thanks to all who contributed recipes for this book!

Index

Index (continued)

Index (continued)

Index (continued)

WISCONSIN COOK BOOK

Favorite Old World, regional and contemporary recipes from the best cooks throughout Wisconsin! Delicious recipes for Wisconsin's bountiful fruit, fresh produce, wild game, fish and fowl. Plus fascinating historical and state trivia!

5 1/2 x 8 1/2 — 112 pages . . . $6.95

IOWA COOK BOOK

Recipes from across America's heartland. From *Indian Two-Corn Pudding* to *Pork Chops Braised in White Wine* this cookbook presents home-grown favorites and encompasses both ethnic traditions and gourmet specialties. A special section entitled "Iowa Corn Recipes" highlights this state's most famous export.

5 1/2 x 8 1/2 — 96 pages . . . $6.95

IDAHO COOK BOOK

Great Idaho recipes from the kitchens of homemakers, Bed-and- Breakfasts and author Janet Walker *(Washington Cook Book, Oregon Cook Book)* offer the opportunity to enjoy Idaho's bounty. From fresh farm produce to fruits and berries, fish and wild game, you will find great recipes for every occasion! Includes Idaho facts, festivals and events.

5 1/2 x 8 1/2 — 96 pages . . . $6.95

COLORADO COOK BOOK

Bring a taste of Colorado to your dinner table! Sample fishermen's fillets, gold miners' stews, Native American and Southwestern favorites, vegetarian feasts and skiers' hot toddies! Recipes, facts and folklore about Colorado.

5 1/2 x 8 1/2 — 128 pages . . . $6.95

WYOMING COOK BOOK

From Yellowstone National Park to Cheyenne, this great collection of recipes will tempt your palate. Wild game, fish, garden fresh vegetables, bison BBQ and many more. Recipes from pioneers, homemakers, and chefs. Includes Wyoming facts.

5 1/2 x 8 1/2 — 96 pages . . . $6.95

ORDER BLANK

GOLDEN WEST PUBLISHERS

☼ 4113 N. Longview Ave. • Phoenix, AZ 85014

www.goldenwestpublishers.com • **1-800-658-5830** • FAX 602-279-6901

Qty	Title	Price	Amount
	Apple Lovers Cook Book	**6.95**	
	Arizona Cook Book	**6.95**	
	Best Barbecue Recipes	**6.95**	
	Chili-Lovers Cook Book	**6.95**	
	Chip and Dip Lovers Cook Book	**6.95**	
	Colorado Cook Book	**6.95**	
	Easy RV Recipes	**6.95**	
	Idaho Cook Book	**6.95**	
	Indiana Cook Book	**6.95**	
	Iowa Cook Book	**6.95**	
	Joy of Muffins	**6.95**	
	Michigan Cook Book	**6.95**	
	New Mexico Cook Book	**6.95**	
	Ohio Cook Book	**6.95**	
	Oregon Cook Book	**6.95**	
	Pumpkin Lovers Cook Book	**6.95**	
	Texas Cook Book	**6.95**	
	Washington Cook Book	**6.95**	
	Wisconsin Cook Book	**6.95**	
	Wyoming Cook Book	**6.95**	
Shipping & Handling Add:	United States $4.00 Canada & Mexico $6.00—All others $13.00		

☐ My Check or Money Order Enclosed

☐ MasterCard ☐ VISA

Total $ _____

(Payable in U.S. funds)

Acct. No. _____ Exp. Date _____

Signature _____

Name _____ Phone _____

Address _____

City/State/Zip _____

Call for a FREE catalog of all of our titles

9/04   **This order blank may be photocopied**   Michigan Ck Bk